NOTES ON STABLE MANAGEMENT IN INDIA AND THE COLONIES

NOTES ON STABLE MANAGEMENT IN INDIA AND THE COLONIES

J. A. NUNN

GYAN

Published by

Gyan Publishing House
5, Ansari Road
Daryaganj, New Delhi-110002
Phone: 011-47034999, 9811692060
E-mail: books@gyanbooks.com

Distribution Network
gyanbooks.com
India, USA, Canada, UK, Australia

ISBN: 978-93-7447-468-6 (PB)

First Published, 1897

2nd Impression 2026

Printed at: Gyan Press, Delhi.

NOTES ON STABLE MANAGEMENT IN INDIA AND THE COLONIES

Author: J. A. NUNN

Notes on Stable Management.

a

NOTES ON
STABLE MANAGEMENT

IN INDIA AND THE COLONIES.

BY

VETY.-CAPT. J. A. NUNN, F.R.C.V.S., C.I.E., D.S.O.,

ARMY VETERINARY DEPARTMENT,

LATE PRINCIPAL LAHORE VETERINARY COLLEGE.

SECOND EDITION, REVISED AND ENLARGED,

WITH A GLOSSARY.

LONDON:

W. THACKER & CO., 2, CREED LANE.

CALCUTTA: THACKER, SPINK & CO.

1897.

PREFACE.

THE first edition of these notes, which was written in India, having been sold out in a much shorter space of time than I ever anticipated when I wrote it, I am induced to offer this to the public. The scope of the original pamphlet has been adhered to, and all that is aimed at is to give the new arrival in the East some idea as to the management of his horses, especially those who are setting up a stable for the first time. The first edition was written in India for Anglo-Indians, who are familiar with native terms; but to this, being published in England, I have added a glossary of the more ordinary Hindustani words likely to be of use. The spelling of these will be probably found fault with by the Oriental scholar; but I have endeavoured to bring it as near the sound as possible, as it is only intended for persons in absolute ignorance of the vernacular. There appearing to be a demand for the book in the colonies, at the suggestion of the publishers I have added a few remarks on Australia and South Africa. The entire work has been rewritten, and the matter contained is the result of my own personal observations during eighteen years' service in India and the colonies at both military and civil duties.

JOSHUA A. NUNN.

LONDON,
March, 1897.

PREFACE TO THE FIRST EDITION.

THE following notes on Stable Management were originally delivered in a lecture to the Officers, Non-Commissioned Officers, and Troopers of the Punjab Light Horse, and as they were considered by the members of the corps to be useful, at their request I have put them on paper. There is no attempt at anything beyond the most elementary rudiments of horse-keeping in India, and all they are intended for is to give volunteers of mounted corps, who have not previously owned horses, some slight idea as to what should be done for the care of their chargers, and not leave them entirely in the hands of native syces and horse-keepers.

JOSHUA A. NUNN.

LAHORE,
December, 1895.

CONTENTS.

FOOD.

WATER.

Air and Ventilation.

Grooming, Stable Gear, etc.

Saddlery, Harness, Carriages and Servants.

STABLE MANAGEMENT.

FOOD.

Gram (*chunnah*).

In the north of India the chief food on which horses are fed is gram, the seed of one of the pea tribe of plants. It is a crop that ripens in the beginning of the summer, when it is harvested, and the grain thrashed out by driving cattle over it in a circle. The dry stalks, that are broken up into small pieces, are used for feeding cattle on, and are known as "missa bhoosa," in contradistinction to the stalks of the wheat when submitted to the same process, and which is known as "suffaid," or white bhoosa. The price of gram varies very greatly, according to the locality and season, and is a subject of much speculation and gambling amongst the native community. I have known it as high as 7 seers (14 lbs. weight), and as low as a maund (80 lbs. weight), per rupee. It also varies greatly in quality, depending on the locality in which it is grown and the conditions under which it has been harvested, and is by native grain-sellers known as first and second class gram. Good gram, when a small quantity is taken up and examined in the palm of the hand, should be free from sand, dirt, small pieces of stick, straws, or other sorts of seeds; in fact, it should, what is known in the trade, "run clean." Each individual grain should be round and plump, as if the husk was well filled. It should not be shrivelled up and wrinkled, and be free from worm or weevil marks, which can be told by there being a small round hole in it, and the grain, when cracked, being found hollowed out and eaten away. Generally the weevil (kirim) will be found in the cavity, but if not, it will be full of a fine powder. Weevil-eaten gram cannot be mistaken, and denotes that the grain is old, and has been badly stored. In most samples of gram, unless quite new, a small proportion of worm-eaten grains will be found, and this is not of any consequence; but if there are a large number, there will be a larger proportion of husk (which has no nourishing properties) than grain, and a larger quantity will have to be given. When a grain of gram is crushed between the teeth it should impart the taste of a dry pea in the mouth, and be devoid of all mustiness, which is present if it has got wet or mouldy, as it is very apt to do. In new gram the husk at the point is of a slightly greenish shade, that disappears with keeping. It is generally supposed that new gram is not so good as when it is a few months old; but myself, I have never seen any ill effects from its use. The only thing to be careful about is that it is perfectly ripe, for natives have a great trick of cutting and plucking every grain, fruit, and vegetable before they have arrived at full maturity. Gram should be crushed or bruised, not *ground*, so as to break the outer husk and allow the juices of the stomach to act on the kernel. It should be crushed or bruised only, as if ground into a fine powder a good deal goes to waste. It is sufficient if each seed is so crushed that it is split in two. Gram, wheat, and all other grains in the East are ground by the women of the family between two stones, one of which revolves on the top of the other by means of a wooden handle fixed in it. To crush gram the stones require to be sharper set than if they are to grind any other grain into flour. Gram can be got ready crushed from the corn-dealer (baniah) at a small increased charge per maund (80 lbs.), or what I generally do is to pay my head groom (syce) the regular bazaar rate (nirrick), and get the women of his family to crush it, they providing their own mill (chuckie). The only disadvantage of this plan is that it is necessary to weigh the grain a second time after it has been crushed, otherwise it will be short, as natives eat it themselves. But I found in the long run the syces would not steal it; natives are sharp enough to see when any profit can be made, and it was not to their advantage to give back short weight. Excellent gram-crushing machines, working with fluted rollers, are sold by several firms in India, and are adjustable so as to take any grain. They are made to fit into a box for travelling, which, when in use, forms a stand for the crusher to work on. They are, however, somewhat expensive, and although admirable for a large stud of horses, are hardly required for a private stable. If, however, expense is no object, they are certainly preferable to the native mill, as they are cleaner, bits of grit not coming off the stone, and each individual grain being crushed, which even the best native mills will not do. Crushed grain is much quicker digested than whole, particularly by old horses whose teeth are not in good order, and who cannot masticate their food properly. It is a common mistake to give too much gram or other grain, there being a prevailing idea that the more that is given the more work the horse will do. There is no greater error; it is like putting more coal into the furnace of an engine that can only consume a certain amount; the extra quantity only goes to waste, and upsets the digestive functions of the stomach. What is required is a judicious admixture of food given at a proper time; not a large quantity improperly given of an improper quality. Gram should be given in the proportion of one part of bran to two of gram; or what is better, one part each of bran (choker), gram, and parched barley (adarwah), or oats (jai), by weight. These can be purchased separately from the corn-dealer and mixed together, and thus cannot be eaten by any of the servants, like pure gram can be. If the horse is not digesting his food properly, whole grains will be found in his droppings that have passed through the bowels unaltered. There will be always a few of these found, especially if the horse is getting parched barley or oats, as the husks of both these grains are very indigestible. If the horse begins to get thin, and fall away in condition as well, it is then time to take some measures to remedy matters, otherwise no notice need be taken.

Barley (*jow*).

In many parts of Northern India, especially on the Afghan frontier, whole, uncrushed barley is used. It does not seem to hurt country-breds, but with old animals that are not used to it, and particularly Australians, the practice is dangerous. During the Afghan War, on one occasion there being no other grain available, whole barley was supplied to the horses of the battery of artillery to which I then belonged. A number of them were attacked with colic, and several died from the irritation caused by the pointed awns or ends of the beards to the bowels. No doubt horses, and particularly young ones, will get used to feeding on most grains if the change is brought about gradually, but a sudden change from any one to another is dangerous. At the best, whole barley is not an economical food. The husk resists the digestive action of the stomach and intestines, and a quantity is always passed out of the body whole. Barley ought certainly always to be crushed, or, better still, parched, and turned into "adarwah." This is done by professional grain parchers in the bazaar; but sometimes, though rarely, some of the women of the servants' families can do it. It consists of half filling a wide shallow iron pan with sand, and placing it over a fire till nearly red hot. A couple of handfuls of the grain is then thrown into the sand with a peculiar turn of the wrist which scatters it over the hot surface, about which it is stirred for a few seconds with an iron spoon or small shovel pierced with holes like a fish-ladle. The grain is partially baked, swells up and becomes brittle, the husk cracking, when it is scraped up and lifted out with the ladle, the sand being riddled through back into the pan. A good parcher will turn out a "maund" (80 lbs.) in a wonderfully short space of time, the whole process being gone through with a dexterity only acquired by long practice. In India barley usually runs very light, there being a great deal of husk. Boiled barley is a most useful diet for a sick horse. It requires well boiling for at least half an hour, and the water then drained off. I have known horses drink this barley-water when they won't look at anything else.

Bran (*choker*).

In most of the large stations in India there are flour-mills in which wheat is ground with the latest machinery, and when obtained from them, bran differs but little from what is seen in England; but in smaller places wheat is ground by native mills, and then the bran is not so clean. When native-made bran is run over the hand, it will be seen that there is a large amount of flour in it, which adheres to the skin like a white powder, and which makes it much more nourishing than the cleaner prepared article. The scales also of native-made bran are much more irregular in size than the European manufactured article. Bran should have a clean, fresh smell about it, and the newer it is the better; if kept long it is likely to get mouldy. This is particularly the case during the rainy season, when the atmosphere being saturated with moisture, a good deal is absorbed by the bran, and if kept in this state for any time will get mouldy. On this account, if it is necessary to store bran during the rainy season, it should be kept in tin boxes. The inside lining of old packing cases, in which perishable goods are brought out from England, do well for this purpose, and plenty can be got for a small sum in the bazaar shops; or, if not, any native tinsmith will make a box out of old kerosine oil tins for a small sum.

Bran Mash.

It is a good plan, particularly in warm weather, in any country to give horses a bran mash once a week, and if one particular evening is fixed upon, syces get into the habit of giving it regularly without special orders. I generally used to give a standing order to give it on Saturday night, for, as a rule, the horses are not required on Sunday. Bran has a slightly relaxing effect, that in warm climates is particularly beneficial. Bran mash is made by simply putting the necessary quantity of bran into a bucket, pouring boiling water gradually on to it, at the same time stirring it round with a stick until the whole is moist and mixed together. The bran should only be damped sufficiently to make it stick together, and should not be sloppy and wet. Some horses at first will not eat bran, but they can be tempted to by mixing a handful of whatever grain they have been used to with it.

Oats (*jai*).

Oats are now largely grown over the Punjab, Northern India, and in Tirhoot, and are sold at nearly the same price as barley. In the seaport towns Australian oats can usually be obtained; and as good oats are grown in the colonies as any part of the world. They are more expensive than the native article, and are generally only used for training race-horses on. The Indian oat, compared with the English, Australian, or South African, is a poor article, running very light, with a great amount of husk; but if properly crushed, and mixed with gram and bran in proportions of one part of each, they are greatly superior to barley. The oat in India is a winter crop, and is harvested in the spring. Both colonial and Indian oats are always white. I have never seen the black or tawny variety which is so common in Ireland. A demand having arisen for them by Europeans, it is sometimes possible in Northern India to buy them in the bazaar; but generally it is necessary to make a special arrangement with the grower, as natives do not use them as a feeding grain for their own animals. They grow the crop round the wells, and cut it green in the straw as forage for the well and plough bullocks in the spring, when they are working hard. Arrangements can generally be made with the cultivator to purchase so much from him by weight, thrashed and delivered at your own stable, or else to purchase so many acres of the standing crop as it is growing; but the former plan is the most satisfactory, as it is astonishing the heavy crop that will be produced;

and, on the contrary, you will be equally astonished to find with the other plan how light it is. The negotiations for the supply of oats should be entered into in good time in the spring—say about the beginning of March—as it is astonishing how slow such matters progress in the East, and they had better be left in the hands of your head syce. No doubt you will be cheated out of a small amount, but you must make up your mind for this before arriving in the East; but you will have the satisfaction of knowing that if you tried to carry on negotiations yourself you would be cheated out of more. I have tried both plans, and found that the syce could drive a better bargain for both of us than when I attempted to deal direct with the cultivator.

Maize (*makkai*).

Although grown all over India, maize is not much used for feeding horses; but in South Africa, where it is known as "mealies," it is the staple food grain for both man and beast. In India it is said to make horses fat and soft, but no animal in the world does harder work than a South African post-cart horse. In all probability the reason they do well on maize is that in the oat-hay forage they get there is a considerable quantity of grain; and although I have never seen it used, the experiment of feeding on oats and maize would be worth while trying in India. In South Africa maize is usually given whole, but in any of the towns it can be obtained crushed, and it is better to give it in this state. During the Afghan War maize was plentiful in some parts of the country, and I gave it to some of the horses that I had charge of. I had it parched on hot sand, in the same way as barley (adarwah) is parched, making it into American pop-corn. With certain somewhat thin and debilitated animals it had a marked effect in getting flesh on them, and all horses eat it greedily. In India maize is a summer crop, ripening in the autumn, when the ears or cobs are picked off the stalks. It is stored in the cob, and the individual grains knocked off as required by rapping them against a stick; but they must be turned over in the heap occasionally, as rats and mice are likely to cause damage, particularly the musk rat, that taints everything it comes into contact with. Horses have frequently been brought to me, said to be off their feed, and on inquiry I have found this only to be caused by the grain being tainted by musk rats, and that when a clean feed is offered to them they devour it ravenously. There are in South Africa and America a number of varieties of maize, but in India I only know of two sorts, in one of which the seeds are white and the other yellow, or a deep red colour. I don't think that there is much difference in them as far as horse food goes, but each individual grain should be plump, and fill out the husk well; they should be free from weevils, worms, or the marks of attacks from rats and mice. The husk should be well filled out, and have a shining, pearl-like, glistening appearance, and when let fall on a stone or other hard substance give off a metallic sound. When broken open, the grain inside should be of a pure white colour, and of a pleasant, mealy smell, like fresh flour. If it is discoloured, it denotes that it has been wet and fermented. Maize can be crushed by most grain-crushing machines, also in the native mill (chuckie) if the stones are properly set; but both in South Africa and India the natives pound it in a large wooden mortar made out of the trunk of a tree.

Wheat (*ghehun*).

Although it is not to be recommended as a food, still I have seen wheat used when no other grain could be obtained, and it was a choice of it or nothing at all; and in parts of Australia, and, I believe, America, it is regularly used as a horse food. It is commonly supposed that wheat is almost a rank poison to horses, and will cause fever in the feet; and no doubt with stabled animals in England it will do so, especially as the majority of cases of this nature are from accidents—horses getting loose and gorging themselves with wheat during the night, or when unobserved. With animals standing out in the open and working hard, as they do in India and the colonies, it is not so dangerous. I should not suddenly change a horse's feed from oats or gram to a full ration of wheat; but when nothing else can be got, it can be given in a small quantity without much fear of danger; but as soon as any other grain could be obtained, it should be used.

Rice (*dhan*).

In Eastern Bengal and Assam horses are fed on unhusked rice and will do well on it. During the expedition into the Lushai Hills in 1879–80, in many places nothing else could be got to feed the transport mules on. Gram is not grown in that part of the country, and what little there is has to be imported, and is at a prohibitive price. I found that animals did well enough on an equal mixture of gram and rice, although at first some of them refused it. In Japan rice is the only grain horses get, and the pack ponies of that country are hardy beasts, and appear to work well on it. If the rice can be crushed, it is all the better; and in Bengal and Assam there is no difficulty in getting this done, as it is the food of the people, and they grind it for their own use.

Millet (*bajara*).

The various millets, known in South Africa as "Kaffir-corn," are not often used in India as horse food, but in the Cape it sometimes is. In India the millet is a summer crop harvested in the autumn. The seeds are small, and of a dark or greyish colour. It requires to be crushed before use, as the husk is very hard.

Pulses (*dhal*).

The various species of pulse grains enter largely into the food of the natives of India. Two, known as "mung" and "mote," or "moat," are excellent for getting flesh on thin, debilitated animals. They are both small oblong seeds of an olive green colour, with a very hard husk, and can be obtained in any bazaar. I prefer the mote to the mung.

They both require to be well boiled to the consistency of a jelly before use, and then being well mixed in with the food, about a pound in weight of the raw seed being enough for each feed, so that the horse gets three pounds daily, a corresponding quantity of the other grain being withdrawn. I have seen most excellent results in weak animals recovering from a debilitating illness from its use, but great care must be taken that it is boiled properly.

Linseed (*ulsie*).

Linseed can be obtained all over India. In fact, a good deal of what is on the English market comes from the East. Under certain conditions it is useful in putting on flesh, and as a diet for convalescents; but care must be exercised in its use, as it contains a great deal of oil, and in cases of sickness with liver complications, which are common in a hot climate, especially in English and Australian horses, it is to be avoided. It has to be boiled to a jelly before use, or, better still, soak it in cold water for some hours until soft, and then boil it. In the hot weather, however, I prefer to use either the "mote" or "mung" to linseed.

Linseed Cake (*rhal* or *khal*).

Linseed cake can be obtained in nearly every large town, and is the residue left after the oil is expressed; but as this process is imperfectly performed, a good deal of oil is left—much more than in the steam-pressed English cake. It is sold by the "seer" (2 lbs. weight), but in irregular lumps, not moulded into cakes as in Europe. Care must be taken in buying it, as it is very likely to be musty, and adulterated with mustard or rape seed. Both these can be easily detected by the taste or smell, leaving a pungent odour and a sharp burning taste behind. The best plan is to crush a small quantity of the cake and drop it into some boiling water, when the sharp smell and taste characteristic of the mustard and rape oil will be given off. A small quantity of linseed cake in the food will fatten horses tremendously, but makes them soft in condition. It is one of the articles used by native dealers to fatten horses for sale, and at this they are most expert. When crushed it can be mixed with the food, or boiled to make linseed tea for sick horses; and for this latter purpose I prefer it to linseed, as there is less oil in it, the smell of which sometimes nauseates an animal and causes him to refuse it.

Black Gram (*cooltee*).

In the Madras Presidency and Southern India black gram is used, the Bengal white gram not being grown there. This has to be boiled before use. Military horses are fed on it, but it is said that it makes them soft. I have, however, no personal experience of black gram.

Preparation of Food.

In India it is the custom to damp the food before it is given. It should not be saturated so as to turn it into a sloppy paste, but just damped sufficiently to make the particles stick together. Grooms (syces) generally deal out each feed into a bucket dry from the corn-bin, and then damp it; but a better plan is to weigh out the whole of the amount required for all the horses, and put it into a wide-mouthed earthen bowl called a "naund," that can be purchased for a few pence, or a box, such as an old wine case, and damp the whole amount together, then portioning it out for each animal. The reason of this is that, if the grain is damped in the buckets, they are at once taken away, and, the probabilities are, never cleaned; but if they have to be brought forward for each feed to be put into them, and the owner takes the trouble now and again to inspect them, "syces," who are creatures of habit, get into the way of cleaning them before they bring them forward. The box, or naund, in which the grain is damped being stationary, can be looked at any time. It is necessary to be very careful about this, as the particles of food left very quickly ferment in a hot climate, and get sour, and quickly taint all the rest. As a rule, about ten minutes is long enough to damp grain; and this should be done as soon before feeding as possible, otherwise, if left long standing, it will get sour. If a horse refuses his feed, it should be at once thrown away, and on no account be kept till the next meal, by which time it is pretty certain to have fermented.

Horses refusing Food.

Some horses are delicate feeders naturally, and take a long time in eating, or refuse their food altogether. In the case of a delicate or slow feeder, the food should be given in small quantities and often, rather than in the usual somewhat rather large feeds three times a day; and the horse should be fed by himself. This is easily done in India, as nearly all stables are loose boxes; but if the animal is picketed out with others that are likely to teaze him, he should be taken away and fed out of a bucket in the "compound" (garden or enclosure round the house). "Syces," like all natives of India, have no idea of the value of time; and if he has his "hooka" (pipe), and a friend to talk to about the price of food-stuffs, rates of wages, and other such-like interesting bazaar topics, he is perfectly content to sit holding the bucket before the horse all day long, if necessary. If the animal refuses his food altogether, then it should be taken away, for if left standing in front of him he breathes on it, and if it remains any considerable time it becomes sour and fermented, and he gets disgusted with it; whereas, if taken away and nothing more given till next feeding-time, the appetite often returns, and the food is consumed with a relish; especially in the warm weather, if he is first led out and exercised, or picketed out under a tree. On no account should the feed that has been refused be kept over till the next feeding-time; a fresh one should be prepared, as in a hot climate wet grain ferments and turns sour in a very short space of time.

Times of Feeding.

The stomach of the horse is very small in proportion to the size of his body, and he requires to be fed often, and in small quantities. In England hunters are fed four, or even five, times a day. In India it is the usual custom to feed three times, and perhaps it is often enough. In all military stations a gun is fired at noon, and the midday feed is given at that hour; but the morning and evening one varies with the season of the year. I usually give only half a feed in the evening about five o'clock, and the remainder the last thing at night, about eight or nine, according to the season of the year; but, unless carefully watched, "syces" will not do this, as it is the custom only to feed three times daily, and "dastour"(custom) is a thing it is impossible to make a native break through.

Bolting Food.

Some horses have a trick of bolting their food without masticating it properly, especially if another is being fed in their company. It is a good plan to feed such horses apart from any others, which can easily be done in an Indian stable, as they are all loose boxes, or, if picketed out in the open, by moving him a short distance away from the others. A small quantity of chaff, grass, straw, or what is known as "bhoosa," which is wheat straw that is crushed and broken into small pieces in the process of treading out the grain by bullocks, mixed in with the feed, will usually make them masticate it properly.

Spilling Food on Ground.

Horses have also a trick sometimes of throwing their food out of the bucket or manger, and spilling a quantity on the ground. Not only is a large amount wasted, but when the animal has finished what is left, and tries at his leisure to gather up what is on the ground, he eats a large amount of earth and dirt with it, which is injurious. The best way I know to prevent this is to feed the horse on a cloth on the ground; any bit of old sacking about four feet square will answer for the purpose.

Grass.

In India hay is not often seen, and horses are fed on grass; even race-horses are trained on it. This may at first sound strange, but Indian grass is very different to English meadow grass, and chiefly consists of the roots and runners, the actual blade of grass not being more than about an inch long. The best grass is what is known as "dhoob." It is a short grass, with long roots and suckers, which is dug up out of the ground with a short iron hoe or trowel, called a "kurpa," which is used with a scraping motion of the hand, the process being called "cheeling." A considerable quantity of earth is taken up with it, which ought to be knocked off against the hoe; but as the grass is sold by weight, and the usual quantity a private "grass-cutter" is supposed to bring in daily is 20 seers (40 lbs. weight), it is not to his advantage to clean it. If horses eat dirty grass for any length of time, the sand and dirt, besides damaging the teeth, is likely to accumulate in the intestines and give rise to what is known as sand colic. When the "grass-cutter" brings in his bundle of grass that he has collected, which he generally does at midday, it should be spread out and cleaned; sticks and thorns should be picked out, as they are likely to lodge in the horse's throat and choke him, and it should be well beaten with a stick to get rid of the sand and dirt. A good plan is to fasten a net between the wooden framework of a "charpoy," or native bedstead, lay the grass on it, and beat it there with a stick, and it is surprising what a quantity of rubbish will fall through. An old lawn tennis net, if the meshes are not too big, answers well for this purpose. Grass-cutters are fond of wetting the grass to make it weigh. If it is brought in fresh, and damped with clean water beyond the actual loss in weight, I do not know that it does much harm; but it is exceedingly likely that the water has been obtained from some stagnant dirty puddle, and the bundle has been left standing for some time so that fermentation has set in, giving it an unpleasant smell. It is therefore best to have the bundles at once opened out and spread in the sun to dry as soon as they are brought in, and not allow the "grass-cutters" to take them away to their own houses. In parts of the foot hills of the Himalayas ("hurriarie," or "hurrialie") grass is obtained. It is not found in the plains, or in the very high mountains where it is cold. It is a long grass, running to about three feet high, and is cut with a curved sickle. When young and green it is a capital fodder grass; but when the seed is shed, and it gets dry, it is unfit for any other purpose than bedding, as the stalks get very hard and brittle, and so dry that there is little or no nourishment in it. It should not then be allowed into the stable for any other purpose than bedding; but being much easier to collect than "dhoob" grass, the "grass-cutters" will bring it as long as they are allowed to, even when it resembles nothing more than a bundle of sticks. I have frequently heard owners of horses in the hills complain of their animals getting thin and out of condition, the cause of which on inquiry was simply due to the bad dry hurrialie grass that was brought for them to eat.

Churrie.

This is the dried stalk of one of the shorgum tribe of plants, which is also known as the Chinese sugar-cane. It is a summer crop cut in the autumn. It grows to five or six feet high, and is cut and stored by the natives as a fodder for the cattle. It would to the new-comer appear to be a most unsuitable article of food, but is full of saccharine matter, tasting quite sweet when chewed in the mouth, so much so that in parts a rough sugar is extracted from it, but to look at is like a bundle of dried reeds. Animals of all sorts are very fond of it, and I have frequently fed my horses on it for days together in out-of-the-way places where no grass was to be obtained. It is not used as a regular horse fodder, but it does well for it on a pinch.

Bhoosa.

In the East all grain is threshed out by the primitive process of putting it in a circle and driving bullocks round on it, and in this process the grain is trodden out of the ear, the straw being split and broken up by the animals' feet into small fragments from one-eighth to two or three inches in length, which is called "bhoosa." This is the staple food of the working cattle, and is also used for horses. It is a most important item of the crop, and in the rural economy of an Indian village almost as much is thought of it as the grain itself. Wheat and barley straw makes what is called "white bhoosa," and gram and the various pulses "missa bhoosa." Both these can be used as horse food; in fact, on the Afghan frontier they get nothing else, and many natives feed their animals entirely on it, never giving them grass; but although they will eat it, and for a time keep condition, it is not to be recommended. If it has to be used, and it is possible to obtain any grass, they should be mixed together. A small quantity of "bhoosa" mixed in the feed will make a greedy feeder masticate it. "White bhoosa" looks like badly chopped straw-chaff. "Missa bhoosa" is of a dark colour, the particles not being straight-like sticks, but bent about, and frequently there are a quantity of the leaves of the plant mixed with it. Care should be taken that both sorts are not mouldy, which is very apt to be the case, as the native farmers store it in large quantities during the winter, and when the new crop comes on, if there is any of last year's left, it is what they try and sell. Being stacked in the open, it is exceedingly likely to get damaged by the rain. "Bhoosa" should have a clean, fresh smell like sweet straw, not be discoloured or have any patches of mould about it, and be free from impurities such as sticks, thorns, or pieces of mud or stones.

Bamboo Leaves (*bāns*).

In Eastern Bengal, Assam, and parts of Burma, the green leaves and young shoots of the bamboo are used for forage. During the Chin-Lushai Expedition in 1889-90, the animals with the force got nothing else for nearly eight months. I had three ponies of my own that were worked moderately hard the whole time, and they remained in good condition. The transport mules, which were worked very hard indeed in a very trying climate, did not fall away nearly as much as I expected. The young shoots and leaves are cut with a sort of a billhook, called a "dah," and care must be taken that only the young green leaves and soft tender shoots are given, the old leaves and the edges of the dry stumps of the bamboo cutting like a razor. I have seen some bad wounds on the lips, tongue, and angles of the mouth from this cause. It is best to make the "syces" and "grass-cutters" pluck the leaves off the branches altogether, and not leave them about the stable, for fear of wounding the horses. This they will readily do, as they use the *débris* for fuel. I have seen some bad cuts and injuries in both men and animals from the edges of the split bamboo, which are very sharp—so much so that the savage tribes on the eastern frontier use a properly split piece of bamboo for a knife in skinning animals; and the sap of the green bamboo appears to have a peculiarly irritating or poisonous action, a wound caused by it festering and suppurating in both man and beast, whereas one inflicted with a dry bamboo will heal up healthy. Horses require a larger amount of bamboo leaves than grass. If an animal is getting 20 lbs. of green "dhoob" grass daily, he will require 30 lbs. of bamboo leaves to keep him in condition. Although at first horses may refuse them, they take to them kindly after a little while.

Oat Hay Forage.

In the South African colonies grass hay is almost unknown. The oat is cut when about half ripe, dried, and given in the straw, in which condition it is known as forage, and is excellent feeding. It is usually sold in bundles, wholesale at so much per hundred, and retail at hotels and livery stables at so many bundles for a shilling. Some years ago, when I was travelling in the Dutch part of South Africa, in the more out-of-the-way parts of which there are no hotels, it was the custom to ask the owner of the farmhouse where you arrived permission to "off-saddle" if you were riding, or "out-span" if driving, for the night or a couple of hours, as the case might be. This was a roundabout way of asking if he could put you and your animals up for the night. When leaving in the morning, it would have been a great breach of good manners to ask for your bill, but you inquired what you were indebted to his head-boy for the forage your horses had consumed—a polite way of asking for your account; the number of bundles per shilling varying according to the time you remained, and the accommodation you had received; but, notwithstanding this fiction, I did not, as a rule, find the total any less than in a regular hotel where you get your bill.

Hay.

Hay, as is known in Europe and Australia, is never seen in India. In some parts, what is called hay can be obtained; but, compared to English meadow hay, it is at the best but poor stuff. No doubt hay of a very tolerable quality can be made in India; in fact, I have done so, but usually the grass is cut after the plant has flowered, the seed ripened and shed, when it is what is known as "the sap being down," and then it is dry and with little nourishment in it. It is generally also allowed to lie out too long after it has been cut in a hot, powerful sun, which utterly bakes it up. The grass should be cut when the seed is green and the sap well up in it, and should not be allowed to remain too long drying. I have generally found that from eight to ten hours of the Indian sun was enough, so that grass cut in the morning should be stacked at night; it will then not be utterly dried up, and in the stack will undergo the process of fermentation that gives the characteristic smell to English hay. There is a certain amount of difficulty in doing this. The grass flowers and seeds at the end of the hot weather, about September, when the monsoon rains are on, and these sometimes last for days together. It is, therefore, sometimes difficult to get a fine day to cut and save the hay in before the seed is shed; and before the dry weather again sets in the sap has gone down, and there is but little nutriment left in the grass. It is not a bad plan to sprinkle some salt over each layer of hay as the stack is made up;

horses eat this cured hay with great relish. In making up the stack, a bundle or two of straw, put on end from the bottom upwards, should be built into the centre of it as it is being raised up, to act as a chimney or ventilator to carry off the heat while the stack is fermenting. If this is not done, there is danger of its catching fire; and even if it should not heat to such a degree, part is likely to get discoloured—what is termed "mow-burned." This chimney can be made with bundles of sticks, boards, or even stones; but sick horses will often eat the straw from the centre of a haystack when they won't look at anything else, and it sometimes comes in useful, and in any event, is not wasted. The stack should be built on a foundation of brambles, stones, or a mud platform — the latter being the best—to raise it and protect it from damage by the rains, which at times come in a regular flood, and also to keep out rats, mice, and other vermin. When the stack gets down to the bottom, care should be exercised in handling it, as it is a great refuge for snakes, and I have seen one fatal accident from snake bite from this cause. It, then, is a good plan to make the men remove the hay in small quantities at a time with a hay-fork, which is easily made by fastening a couple of short sticks converging from each other on to a long bamboo; but natives are such fatalists that, no matter how much warned of the danger they are incurring, they will not take the commonest precautions as to their safety if it gives them a little extra trouble. A somewhat larger quantity of dry grass is required than green "dhoob" by weight, the proportion being about 15 to 20 lbs. respectively.

Green Food (*khawid*, or *khasil*).

In the spring of the year in India it is common to give horses green wheat, oats, or barley. This is cut in the straw from the time it is about a foot high until the grain begins to ripen, a period that lasts about a month or six weeks in the Punjab—from the middle of February till the end of March. This green food is called by the natives "khawid," or "khasil." It has an excellent effect on the system, and is what is used by the native dealers to get their horses into condition for sale. Too large a quantity should not be given at first, as it is likely to cause diarrhœa; about 4 lbs. daily being sufficient at first, but it may be increased up to double this amount if it agrees with the animal. Care should be taken that the green food is only given when young and the straw tender, for when it gets ripe, and the straw woody and hard, it is very indigestible, and a common cause of intestinal obstruction and colic. In some parts green barley is given in the same manner, and when it is young it is as good as wheat or oats; but when it begins to ripen it should be stopped, as the awns or beards begin to get hard, and not only are they likely to choke the horse, but to cause dangerous intestinal obstruction. Oats can be given much longer than barley or wheat; in fact, as I have said, ripe oats are cut in the straw, and used as hay in many parts of the world. The green crop must be purchased standing from a cultivator, and this is best arranged through your head "syce." It is sold by measurement, a patch in the field being marked out; or else the grass-cutters go and cut as much as is required daily, the whole amount used being afterwards measured up and paid for at the fixed bazaar rate, or, as it is termed, the "nirrick."

Green Gram.

Natives are very fond of giving horses green gram, but it is a most dangerous custom. It is most indigestible, the stalk when green being full of a strong tough fibre. The sap and leaves have a peculiar irritating or almost corrosive property, and in the spring of the year many fatal cases of intestinal disease are caused by it.

Carrots (*gajar*).

Carrots are plentiful all over Northern India. They come on in the spring, and are an excellent green food. They can be bought very cheaply, and if kept in a cool, dry place, can be stored for a considerable time; but they require to be turned almost daily, or they will get rotten. When used they should either be washed to remove the earth, or, as in the East this is quite dry, knocked with a stick to remove it. They should be given whole, or else cut into long slices, not across into lumps. This latter practice is dangerous, as horses are thus inclined to bolt them whole, and the short round lump is likely to stick in the throat and cause choking.

Lucerne.

Lucerne grows well all over Northern India, and although not cultivated by the natives for their own use, they know perfectly well what it is, and call it by the English name. In most of the towns where there are any Europeans collected together, it is usual to grow it in the Government or station garden, from where it can be purchased retail. Some native corps, who remain some time in the one place, also grow it for the benefit of the regiment, and sometimes it is possible to obtain some from them; but as a rule they only have enough for their own use. Round the large military cantonments in some places, the neighbouring farmers, finding that there is a demand for it, have taken to growing it for sale, and it can be bought in the bazaar; but as the supply is not certain, it is better to enter into a contract with one of the growers to supply the quantity by weight daily required. In making this bargain it is best to use the agency of the head "syce," as if it falls short, or is not forthcoming, he can be made responsible; and natives being erratic creatures, it is quite possible that some morning you may be told that there is no more, or that the grower has sold his crop to some one else, perhaps at even a smaller price than you are giving. Whenever there is a well in the compound, and I have been long enough in one place, I have always grown as much as I could for myself. It is easily done, and there is no more useful crop in connection with an Indian stable. In the dry, hot weather the difference in the condition of horses that are getting a fairly liberal supply of green food, and those that are only getting the burned-up grass that is then procurable, is most marked. The only difficulty about growing lucerne is that at first a large supply of water is necessary until the roots strike. If you have a garden, then, of course, you have to keep a pair of bullocks to raise water from the well for irrigation purposes; but if you do not run to this luxury, then a pair of bullocks can be hired for two or three days in the week. The landlord of the house has to keep the well and the Persian wheel, by which the water is raised, in order, and find the first pair of ropes for it. The tenant has to find the earthen pots, or "chatties," that are fastened on to it, by which the water is raised up. These "chatties" are cheap things enough, but they are easily broken. I always found that the best plan was to provide the first lot myself, and then give a small sum monthly to the gardener to keep them going; and it saved money in the end, as I found that not nearly so many were smashed under this system as when I paid for what were required. If a gardener is regularly employed, it is, of course, part of his business to look after the lucerne bed; but for an ordinary stable of, say, four or five animals, an acre of lucerne will be ample, and a man exclusively for this is not necessary. A gardener can be got for about Rs. 10 a month, but a man can be got to come two or three times a week and look after it for half this. I found, however, that if I gave it to one of the syces, that the women and children of his family would attend to it, as, when once started, it only requires weeding, and that the work was better done than by a professional gardener, unless one was regularly employed. The best seed is the acclimatized English, or the Cabul brought down from Afghanistan. The English seed can be obtained from any seedsman, or the Government Horticultural Gardens at Lahore or Saharunpore, at about a rupee a pound, and this is enough to sow about an acre with, which should be done at the end of the cold weather. If only a small quantity is grown, it is best to sow it on ridges, as it then, no doubt, can be kept free from weeds, and the cost of weeding, on an acre or two, is but trifling; but it is an error to suppose that lucerne cannot be sown broadcast. At the cattle farm at Hissar, in the Punjab, several hundred acres were grown in this way, as the cost of making ridges on such a large quantity of land would have been prohibitive. Of course, this lucerne was not so clean as if it had been grown on ridges, but the cattle picked it out from the weeds when it was put before them. Fresh seed will have to be sown about every three years, and the crop may be cut about five or six times during the season. About 4 lbs. is enough for a horse, but it is best to begin with half this quantity and gradually increase it, as if too large an amount is given at once it is likely to cause colic.

Guinea Grass.

Some years ago this was a very favourite grass forage to grow for horses, but lately lucerne has supplanted it, and, I think, rightly. The advantage of guinea grass is that it lasts through the hottest months of the year, which lucerne does not, but it requires a great deal of water. It grows in separate tufts, and they should be planted some distance apart, or otherwise they will crowd each other out.

Sugar Cane (*gunna*).

Sugar cane is not often used as an actual food, but horses are very fond of it, and on my visits to the stable I usually had some pieces carried after me in a basket when it was in season. It ripens at the end of the summer, and lasts into the winter. It is sold in long sticks, and should be chopped up into pieces; but the servants will steal it, as they eat it themselves as a sweetmeat.

Turnips (*shalgham*).

The ordinary white turnip grows all over the Punjab in the winter, and when carrots are not to be procured, I have used them in their place, preparing them in the same manner. Horses soon learn to eat and relish them.

Salt (*nimmuk*).

Salt is required by all animals in a certain quantity in their food to keep them in health. There are three different varieties sold in the native shops. Rock salt ("putter ke nimmuk"); ordinary salt, which is merely the rock salt crushed and powdered; and black salt ("kali nimmuk"). On the coast sea salt can also be obtained, but it is not to be found far inland. The common custom in India is to give powdered salt in the food, the usual daily allowance being about an ounce. I prefer to leave a lump of rock salt in the manger for the horse to lick when he likes. Some owners have a lump of it hung by a string to the wall, but I do not think this is advisable, as I have known more than one horse turn a wind-sucker from getting into the habit of licking and playing with it.

Tonics.

It is a common supposition, deeply rooted in the minds of horsemen, that, when a horse loses condition, he at once requires a tonic; and an immense number of these and "condition powders" are advertised. There is no better paying speculation in the world than the sale of these articles, as the majority of them consist of a few cheap and simple ingredients, that are retailed to the public at a hundred per cent. their original cost; and the best that can be said about these nostrums is that some of them are innocent and do no harm, while they serve to amuse the owner. The action of a tonic is to stimulate the appetite, and if the horse is feeding well they are certainly useless, if not actually harmful. If the horse feeds, and continues to fall off in condition, the chances are that there is something wrong in the stable management, which should be carefully inquired into. If this only occurs once with one animal, the inference is that medical advice is required, but if several are in the same state, or it is a matter of constant occurrence, then in most cases a change of "syce" is required, and it will be usually found better and cheaper than having recourse to any of these various advertised "cure-alls."

Horses not Feeding.

Horses refuse their food from a variety of causes. It is usually the first symptom noticed in the majority of attacks of illness, and I cannot too strongly urge that in such cases the sooner professional advice is obtained the better, there being nothing in which the old proverb, "a stitch in time saves nine," more applies to. On the other hand, horse owners are inclined to get very anxious without cause about horses not feeding, and to imagine that because he refuses to feed, or does not finish it up with a good appetite, that the animal is in a dangerous state. Horses are much like ourselves, and we all know that we sometimes do not feel inclined to do justice to a "square" meal, and that if we dine off a plate of soup we feel ready for a good breakfast in the morning. If the horse refuses his feed, or only plays about with it, have it at once removed; at the next only give him a little hay or grass, and the probabilities are that at the next he will eat up his grain with a hearty appetite. If he does not, then the sooner professional advice is called in the better, as you may be certain that something is wrong.

Damaged Food.

Damaged, mouldy, or sour food, the horse, of course, will not eat unless he is very hungry, and then only sufficient to stay his appetite. Damaged grain there is no excuse for, and can only be given through carelessness or indifference on the part of the owner or his servants. Sour food, or food that has fermented, is, with the best intentions, likely to be placed before the animal, as it is surprising how soon fermentation will set up in damp grain in a hot climate. The food should not be damped more than twenty minutes or half an hour at the most before it is given, and a dirty bucket will easily contaminate it. In the hot weather in India, particularly during the rains, when both man and beast are down below par, very little will put both off their feed. If the food, however, is at all sour it ought to be at once detected, as the smell is unmistakable.

Irregular Teeth.

In old horses the back teeth get irregular and worn in such a fashion that the food cannot be masticated and crushed, and is not then properly digested. The upper jaw of the horse is wider than the lower one, so that the upper teeth overlap the lower ones at the outside, and the lower ones the upper at the inside. By continually wearing, the upper back teeth get worn down more on the inside than the outside, and the lower ones more on the outside than the inside, or, in other words, the grinding surface of the teeth, instead of being horizontal, is at an angle or slope. The horse masticates his food with a sideways motion of the jaws, crushing the food between the back teeth like mill-stones, so that if the grinding surfaces of the teeth are not level, but sloped at an angle, they become locked, and prevent sufficient sideways play of the jaws. If this is suspected, the back teeth can be easily inspected by turning the horse with his tail to the sun, grasping the tongue with the left hand and opening the mouth, while the light is reflected into it by a small looking-glass held in the right. They can also be felt by putting one's hand on the outside of the cheek, where the outer edge of the upper teeth can be easily felt, and pushing the finger inwards and upwards, so as to get on the grinding surface when the horse opens his mouth, and the angle they are at can be at once detected through the cheek. This is, of course, only a rough method of examination, but it gives one a fair idea of the state the molars are in. If a tooth is broken or deficient, the corresponding one in the other jaw from not being worn down will become over-grown and fill up the vacant space, even growing so long as to damage the gum or bone in the jaw above or below it, as the case may be, and preventing the horse feeding. If it is one of the front molars, it is possible that the growth may be detected from outside, but the probabilities are that a more careful examination will be necessary, and, at all events, professional skill required to set matters right. Horses also suffer from decayed teeth; and, in fact, the whole matter of equine dentistry is much more important than is usually supposed, many animals remaining poor and thin simply because their teeth are not properly attended to.

Young Horses Cutting Teeth.

Young horses sometimes have great trouble when cutting their teeth, and if they go off their feed they should be attended to; but this requires professional skill.

Quidding.

When young horses begin to what is called "quid" their food, it is almost a certain indication that there is something wrong with the mouth. "Quidding" is gathering up a mouthful of hay or grass, rolling it about in the mouth, and half masticating it till it gets into a lump or ball, and then spitting it out without swallowing it. Sometimes a dozen or more of these "quids" will be found in the manger or on the stable floor.

Indigestion (*bud hazmie*).

Indigestion, or dyspepsia, which horses suffer from more commonly than the public imagine, will put them off their feed; but this is a matter for professional advice and treatment, and it is exceedingly dangerous for the owner to go trying domestic remedies. I have had many fatal cases of bowel diseases brought to me that have arisen solely from this cause.

Lampas.

This is a disorder that is firmly fixed in every groom's mind, both European and native, and is supposed to consist of a swelling or inflammation of the palate, or "barbs," just behind the upper incisor teeth. I do not deny for a moment the existence of such a thing, but what I do maintain is that in 75 per cent. of the cases brought to one, it exists only in the imagination of the attendant. The popular remedy some years ago was to cauterize the part with a hot iron, and I have no hesitation in saying that any one doing this should be indicted for cruelty to animals. Lately, the popular treatment has been more merciful in having the part scarified with a lancet, but even this is useless. Where lampas does exist, there is more or less enlargement and swelling of the membrane of the entire alimentary canal, but the "barbs" of the mouth being the only part visible, it is popularly supposed to be a local affection. Under these conditions, it will be readily understood how utterly useless lancing or scarifying one small part of the affected canal will be. A small dose of aperient medicine, or even putting the horse on a laxative diet of bran mash for a few days, will do all that is required, without having recourse to heroic measures.

Nose-bags (*tobra*).

Nose-bags are sadly neglected by "syces," and unless looked after by the owner, they never dream of cleaning them, so that, particularly with leather ones, they get into a very filthy condition, and frequently horses refuse to eat out of such dirty things. Both mangers and nose-bags should frequently be washed and scrubbed out with soap, or sand and water. Nose-bags are, at the best, a necessary evil, and if they have to be used at all, canvas ones are better than leather, being more easily cleaned. I only allowed nose-bags to be used when on the march, or out in camp; when in the stable the horses were fed out of an ordinary bucket, or else a manger, and even then they were not fastened on the head, but held on the ground.

Mangers (*kurlie*).

In the stable a manger should be used. In an Indian stable one is easily made out of a shallow, wide-mouthed earthen vessel ("gumalo"), built up with mud, about three feet high, in the corner. The "syces" can do this themselves, and the gumalo only costs a few pence in the bazaar. I always had two built in opposite corners, one for food and the other for water. If for any reason the manger cannot be built, or there is not one in the stable, then the horse should be fed out of a tin or zinc bucket, or else off a feeding-sheet. An old gunney-bag, spread out opened at the seams, answers admirably. The "syce" should hold the bucket or sheet while he is feeding, or the horse is very likely to knock the first over, or tear the sheet, by pawing at it with his fore feet.

Worms (*kirim*).

Parasites, or worms, in the intestines cause horses to lose condition very quickly. The most common are long white ones, like ordinary earthworms, about five to eight inches long; and small, very thin thread-like ones, about three inches long. They cause the horse to become very unthrifty and thin, the coat being dull, without the natural gloss that is seen in health, or as it is termed, "hide-bound." The horse is also apt to back up against any projection, or into a corner, and rub his tail against the wall, breaking off the hair, and giving it an unsightly appearance. If worms are suspected, the "syce" should be instructed to look for them in the horse's droppings in the morning, where the long ones are most likely to be found; also to examine under his dock, where the small ones will leave a yellowish incrustation under the root of the tail. An enema of common salt and water, made by dissolving about a table-spoonful of salt in a quart of luke-warm water, generally suffices to get rid of the small ones. The large ones, however, require medical treatment, which should be left in professional hands. If there are any worms passed, the litter, droppings, etc., should be carefully burned, and the floor of the stable scraped and the *débris* burned, and a new floor laid down.

Rubbing the Tail.

Although commonly due to parasites in the intestines, "particularly the small thread-worms," with some horses it is a trick; neglect also, and the irritation caused by dirt, will often cause it. In India it is more often seen in coarse-bred horses, such as many Australians are, than in country-breds and Arabs. If it is from dirt, washing the tail well with soap and water will stop it; if it is a trick, keeping the tail in a tail-case, which is merely a piece of leather, with buckles and straps to fasten it on with; or an ordinary roller bandage put round from the tip to the root will generally stop it.

Scouring (*dāst*).

Scouring, or diarrhœa, is usually seen in nervous horses when they get excited, and, as a rule, disappears when they get quiet again. It is more commonly seen in light-coloured, or what the horseman calls "washey," chestnuts and blacks, than any other colour. Some horses will always scour after a draught of cold water, and with such the chill should be taken off either by adding a little warm water, or standing the bucket out in the sun for a couple of hours before it is used. If the scouring persists, after returning to the stable, let the next feed consist of dry bran, not "bran mash," and this generally stops it. If a horse that is not in the habit of doing so suddenly begins scouring, it is a mistake to try and stop it too suddenly, as frequently it is an effort of nature to throw off something deleterious to the system. If, however, the diarrhœa should continue persistent, then professional advice should be obtained.

WATER.

Water (*pani*).

Horses prefer soft to hard water, and are particularly partial to rain-water. Many horses refuse to drink at all from a running stream, unless very thirsty, and even then will not take as much as is necessary. Mules, which in other respects are hardy animals, are very dainty and particular about their water. Such horses should be watered either out of a bucket or a still pool. In mountain and quick running streams there is often a large quantity of sand and small gravel held in suspension, that sinks to the bottom in places where the current runs slow. I have seen more than one death caused by constantly watering horses in such streams, by the animal swallowing a quantity of such sand; it accumulates in large masses in the intestines, and causes "sand colic." If it is necessary to water horses from such places for any length of time, if a suitable pool cannot be found where the water is still and the sand and gravel can settle, one should be made by building a dam.

Times of Watering.

Horses should be watered half an hour before feeding, or, if this cannot be managed, at least two hours should elapse after the feed before he is allowed to drink his fill. The reason of this is that the hard grain the horse eats is only partly crushed and broken by the teeth, and it is in the stomach where it is principally softened before passing on into the intestines. If, when the stomach is full of partly digested food, a large quantity of water is given, some of it will be washed into the intestine, and, being hard, and not properly softened, irritate it and set up colic. The best plan is to always have water in front of the horse, so that he can drink when he likes, and I have found that they take much less this way than when watered at regular times. In India this can be easily done by building up in mud a wide-mouthed, shallow, earthen vessel, called a "gumalo," in one corner of the stable, in the same way that a manger is made. It should be high enough for the horse to conveniently reach it, and be kept constantly full.

Watering Troughs.

When horses are watered at a trough or stream, as is necessarily the case with military animals, if they are thirsty they push their noses deep into it and drink greedily. They then lift their heads and look round them, and many persons think they have finished. This is not the case, as the horse is merely recovering his breath after his draught, and he should not be taken away until he either turns round and will drink no more, or until he begins to splash the water about with his nose and play with it, which shows he does not want any more.

Watering on a Journey.

It is commonly supposed that when on a journey horses should not be watered, but, in a warm climate, as long as only a steady pace is maintained and only a moderate quantity given, it does not do any harm, and, to judge from one's own experiences, certainly is refreshing. Of course, this must be done in moderation, like everything; and it undoubtedly would be dangerous to allow a horse to drink his fill and then give him a hard gallop directly afterwards; but, in both the South African and Australian colonies, I have travelled some hundreds of miles in post-carts and coaches, and the drivers at pretty nearly every stream they cross pull up and allow the horses to drink a few mouthfuls. I have never heard of any harm coming from this practice, and at the end of the journey they drink far less water than if they had been deprived of it while at work. In Norway, the carriole drivers water their ponies in the same way, and it is icy-cold coming from the glaciers.

Watering after a Journey.

When the journey is completed, it is advisable to walk the horse about for a short time, to allow him to get cool before watering; or, better still, and what every practical horseman will do, is to pull up and allow him to walk the last mile, so that he arrives at his stable fairly cool, and not reeking with perspiration. Grooming also will be greatly facilitated by this.

Watering Bridles (*kazai*).

Watering bridles are generally very much neglected, "syces" (grooms) never seeming to think that they require any care or attention. They are generally a mass of rust and dirt, and having one of these filthy things put into the mouth, is a much more common cause of horses going off their feed than is generally supposed. They are frequently thrown out on the heap of bedding, and left in the sun all day, and when put into the horse's mouth the iron of the bit is burning hot. I consider that this is one of the chief reasons of the sores that so frequently form at the angles of the mouth in the summer months, and which are most troublesome to cure. The bit of the watering bridle should be scrubbed daily with sand until it is polished, and the leather-work cleaned with soap (sabon) or dubbing (momrogan); if this is not done, it very soon perishes with the heat and becomes rotten, and if a horse is at all fresh and plays about, it breaks, the animal gets loose, and a serious accident is the result of the want of a little forethought.

Leeches (*jonk*).

In India leeches frequently get into the nose while the horse is drinking, especially out of ponds and streams, and although they are not absolutely dangerous, they cause troublesome bleeding, and make the animal cough and sneeze. They are sometimes very difficult to get rid off, and the best plan is to place some water in a bucket before the horse and splash it about. The leech is attracted by this, and comes down the nostril, when it can be caught if the operator is quick enough. A handkerchief is necessary, as the leech is too slippery to hold in the fingers. It is generally best to let one of the "syces" do this, promising him a small reward when the nuisance is got rid of, as some of them are wonderfully expert at it, and have untiring patience.

Wells.

In some Indian towns there is a water supply laid on to the houses by pipes, but in the majority it is obtained from a well (khua) in the compound. In these cases a water-carrier ("bheestie") has to be kept to draw and carry water for the household and stables, which he brings in a leather bag; "mussuk," the small leather bucket that he uses to fill the bag with, being called a "dholl." These water-bags should be renewed twice a year, as they get very foul inside if kept much longer, and they are only worth about Rs. 2 each. Very few people ever think of cleaning out the well, but it should be done at least once a year, as it is surprising the amount of rubbish, such as dead leaves and vegetation, gets into it. The landlord of the house should undertake this, but it is generally difficult to get him to do it without the tenant threatening to do it himself and deduct the cost out of the rent. There are professional well-cleaners in Northern India, who will do the work by contract. As a rule, it takes about three days, as the well has to be pumped dry by working the lifting wheel with relays of bullocks day and night, when a man goes down and removes the accumulation of rubbish from the bottom. Care should be taken to first lower down a lighted candle, or throw a bundle of lighted straw down before any one is allowed to descend, as there is frequently an accumulation of foul gas at the bottom, and I have known more than one accident from neglect of this precaution. Unless I had very good reason for knowing that the well had been lately cleaned, I always had this done on going into a new house. If this is neglected, the water during the rainy season is apt to get very foul, and I have known severe outbreaks of illness from this cause both in men and animals.

AIR AND VENTILATION.

Stables.

NOTHING is worse for horses than close, ill-ventilated stables, and in India, where they are made out of such cheap material as mud and sun-dried brick, there is no excuse for their being too small. In some of the newer houses, stables are made out of burned brick; but I prefer the older ones of mud or sun-dried brick, as the walls are generally thicker, and this makes them cooler in the summer and warmer in the winter. It is also of importance that they should not be too low, but of the two evils I should prefer a small stable with a lofty roof to a larger one with a low one, provided there was ventilation in the top. Every stable should have a good deep verandah round it; it not only keeps off the sun in the summer, but is useful to put bedding, etc., in during the rain. If there is no verandah, one can be easily made with the flat straw screens used by natives, called "jamps," and bamboo supports. The doorways should be high and wide, so that there is no danger of the horse hitting his hips or head against it in going in and out. A fractured hip-bone is frequently caused by horses rushing through narrow doorways, and a troublesome disease known as "poll evil" is generally caused by striking the head against too low a one. It is also well to have the sides of the door-posts rounded off, not left at an angle. If there is no window at the back of the stable, opposite the door, one should be made above the horse's head, and another smaller one on a level with the floor, so as to allow the air to circulate freely. If possible, avoid a draught, but always remember that it is better to have plenty of fresh air and a draught than a stuffy stable without one, as the horse can always be kept warm with extra clothing, bandages, and bedding. Thatched roofs are much cooler in summer and warmer in winter than the flat earthen ones that are generally used in Northern India. Indian stables are almost always divided off into loose boxes, the partition walls being continued up to the roof. I think they should be only built high enough to prevent the horses teasing each other over them, as if continued right up they interfere with the free circulation of the air. If this cannot be done, on account of the partitions helping to support the roof, a window should be knocked through in each. In South Africa stables are usually simply a long shed with a manger running down the back wall, without any partitions between the standings, and the horses are simply tied up to a ring in the manger with the head rope. Cape horses are, however, exceedingly quiet, and will stand still all day long. They never seem to think of kicking or biting at each other like the Indian country-bred does.

Chicks.

The plague of flies in the East, particularly during the rains, cannot be realized in England, and if not protected against them, they will almost worry horses to death. For this reason the doors and windows of the stable should be fitted with "chicks," or mats, made out of split bamboos or reeds, with interspaces between them, which allow of light and air passing through, but which will keep the flies out. They are not very costly articles, and add most materially to the comfort of the horse. If carefully looked after, and not let flap about in the wind, they will last for years with a very small annual expenditure for repairs.

Stable Floors.

The stable floor should be made of wet clay beaten down, and left to thoroughly dry. This can be carried out by the "syces," and if thoroughly done, they will last a good many months. I always make it a practice to dig up the floors of stables in a new house, before they are occupied, a foot and a half deep, and thoroughly renew it, and usually it is astounding the amount of foul earth that has to be removed. I also have the whole of the floor picked up and renewed once a year—for choice, at the end of September or beginning of October, after the rains have stopped. Any moisture should be at once removed, before it has time to soak into the floor; or, if it has, the moist earth should be swept away with a broom (jaru), made out of a number of pliable twigs tied together, and fresh dry earth sprinkled over the top of it. A supply of dry powdered earth should be kept outside each stable door in a box ready for use when required. The ordinary earth that is in the compound will not do to make floors out of, although "syces" will use it if allowed, as it is less trouble to get than clay (kicher ke muttee), but it will not bind, and when trodden on breaks up and wears into dust.

Charcoal (*khoalie*).

Although it looks dirty, powdered charcoal sprinkled over the floor has a powerful effect as a deodorizer. The ashes of a wood fire do nearly as well as charcoal for this purpose, and can be obtained anywhere, as wood is universally used for fuel all over India. In some stables earthenware vessels (chatties) are buried under the floor to catch the urine. This is an abominable, filthy custom, and should never be permitted, as there is no more certain cause of disease. Diseases of the feet, such as foul smelling, suppurating frogs, thrush, and canker, are in the majority of cases caused by horses standing on wet, filthy floors.

Picketing.

In the hot season horses should, if possible, be picketed out at night as soon as it gets cool in the evening. It is the greatest relief to an animal to be brought out of a hot stable into the open air, even if the actual temperature is no less than indoors. If the flies or mosquitos are troublesome, the nets sold for the purpose will keep them off. If the net is not sufficient, a fire made out of the stable litter on the windward side will drive them away, and horses do not mind smoke. It is as well to have a regular standing made with mud, in the same way as the stable flooring, as otherwise the ground soon gets broken up and foul. The standing should be swept clean every morning, and mended in the same way as the stable floors are.

Bedding (*bechalie*).

There is nothing better than clean straw for bedding, and it is a great mistake to stint horses in it. If a good deep bed is given, they will lie down and rest themselves, whereas, if there is not enough, and the floor feels hard through it, they will walk about over it, and far more will be wasted than if the horse was lying down on it. The bedding should be taken up every morning, and any soiled straw removed. It should be well shaken up and spread out in the sun to dry and air, and at night, when again put down for use, a small quantity of fresh straw added to it. In wet weather the bedding can be aired and dried in the verandah. All soiled straw and droppings should be at once removed in a basket (tokrie), which should be provided for the purpose; and it is wonderful, if this plan is adopted, how little fresh straw is required to keep the horse constantly supplied with a good bed; and nothing is more saving to the wear and tear of the legs and feet than to get the animal to lie down at night. In Australia and South Africa wheat or oat straw can be obtained, but in India rice straw is generally used, or else the long elephant grass that grows on the banks of rivers and swampy places. Both are good enough for the purpose, only they are brittle, and more is required than when wheat straw is used, as they quickly break up.

Sawdust (*burradah*).

In the north of India the deodar, or Himalayan cedar sawdust, can always be obtained from any of the timber depôts on the banks of the large rivers, almost for the expense of carting it away. It makes a good bed if straw cannot be obtained, but is liable to stick to the horse and get in under his coat if at all long, and gives much more work grooming. It is also more troublesome to remove in the morning to air, and if any wind is blowing a good deal gets wasted. If used, it is best to have it spread out in one stall and leave it there, only using it at night, putting the horse into another during the daytime. Any sawdust that gets damp or soiled should be at once removed, as it very soon begins to smell badly.

Shavings.

Shavings of deodar or pine can also be obtained, but they require to be carefully sorted out, as there are likely to be splinters in them, and in lying down the horse may give himself a bad wound.

Sand (*ret*).

Sand can be obtained anywhere along the banks of the rivers; but it is hard, and does not form a very yielding bed, and I should not use it if anything else could be got. It requires to be sifted, to get rid of the pebbles and stones it contains. If straw is scarce and sand has to be used, the best plan is to put a layer of about a foot of sand over the floor, and a thin layer of straw over it; this will make a much softer bed than the sand alone.

Horses eating Bedding.

This is a trick some horses have, and from which they seldom can be cured. It is generally the custom to put a muzzle (chik-na) on them at night; but this, of course, stops their feeding at all. I prefer to bed them down with sand, sawdust, or shavings, and leave them free to feed at night.

If a muzzle is used, it should be a wire one, not leather, as these get very foul and dirty, and interfere with the horse's breathing, which the wire one does not.

Exercise.

In India it is usual to exercise ordinary hacks, polo ponies, and harness horses, not doing any special work, twice a day—morning and evening. The length of time they are out, and the amount of ground they cover, is very variable—in most cases depending on whether the "syce" is in a mood to take exercise or not himself. They usually take horses out on the road to the bazaar, or some favourite meeting-place; and it is not an uncommon thing to see a couple of dozen horses, belonging to various people, standing about, while their respective "syces" are sitting about, smoking and discussing their masters and various bazaar topics of interest. Under these circumstances the horses do not get much exercise; and many a mysterious injury, that cannot be accounted for, is inflicted by their kicking at each other while standing about in this manner. If the compound is large enough, it is a good plan to make a ring with the stable litter and have the horses exercised round it. You can then be certain they are getting a fair amount of work; but a large ring is necessary, and if there is a garden it spoils the compound. Furthermore, horses get into a very careless, slovenly way of walking when led round and round in this monotonous fashion daily. "Syces" generally lead horses at exercise, and most horse-owners will not allow them to ride; but I think this is a mistake, and if they can ride, I always allow them to do so. If they lead the horse, he will go along in a listless fashion, and walk with his head down, stumbling at every step; whereas, if he is ridden, he will carry his head up and go in a much more lively and collected fashion, and it being much pleasanter for the "syce" to ride than walk, the full amount of exercise is more likely to be taken. "Syces" nearly always ride at exercise bare-backed; but they should be made use a folded blanket as a pad, kept in its place by a body-roller, as the anatomy of the native of India is such that, without any protection, he is likely to give the horse a sore back. They should also only be let use a snaffle bridle, as few know how to handle a double one. When at exercise knee-caps should be worn. These should be bought from a European saddler, and care be taken that the top strap is fitted with a piece of indiarubber in the middle, to allow of its giving with the motion of the limb. If there is not this indiarubber spring, when the top strap is buckled tight enough to prevent the cap slipping down, the motion will cause it to rub the skin at the back of the knee; and I have seen some bad abrasions, that caused temporary lameness, from this cause. If the top strap is buckled loose enough to avoid this chafing, then the knee-cap won't stay up in its proper place, if it has no spring. The country-made knee-caps sold by the native saddlers seldom are fitted with it; and if they are they cannot be relied on, as generally the indiarubber is bad and perished. The lower strap of the knee-cap should be buckled quite loose, it being only required to keep it down and prevent it flapping about; but "syces" are very apt to draw it tight also, and if they do, it is pretty certain to cut the skin.

GROOMING, STABLE GEAR, Etc.

Heel Ropes (*pecharie*).

If possible, horses should be left loose, which generally can be done in India, as most of the stables are loose boxes. Sometimes it is necessary to fasten them up, such as when picketed out at night in the hot weather or on the march. There are several plans of picketing, each having its advantages and disadvantages; but as these generally apply to military animals, I will merely mention those commonly used in private stables. The most common plan is to fasten the horse up with head and heel ropes, to wooden pegs driven into the ground. Heel ropes (pecharie) consist of either two ropes about twelve feet long, ending in a single one, so as to be Y-shaped, the single one being fastened to a wooden peg (make) driven into the ground, and the two arms to the horse's hind fetlocks by means of leather straps, called "muzzumas." These straps are loops of rope covered with leather, to one end of which the heel rope is tied, and into which the hind foot is slipped, being secured by a flat leather thong wound round the middle of it behind the fetlock joint to prevent its slipping off. The strap is then of a fig. 8, or hour-glass shape, the heel rope being tied in one loop, the foot placed in the other, the thong forming the neck or constriction. These, I think, are the best form of leather foot strap; but in buying them care should be taken that the stitching of the leather is on the outside, as if it is on the inside, where natives often put it, it is very likely to rub the skin and cause a bad cracked heel. Another form of "muzzuma" is made out of stiff flat leather lined with felt. This has a slip loop going round it, with a buckle on one side and a strap on the other, that runs along the centre. The heel rope is tied to one end, the foot put into the other, and when the strap is buckled tightly, the running loop is drawn close up to the heel, so as to keep the whole arrangement in its place. This form of "muzzuma" is the usual kind sold; but it is objectionable, as the edges get stiff and hard, and are likely to cut the heel, which the round ones do not. Both sorts of leather "muzzumas" require to be kept soft and pliable with dubbing (momrogan), which "syces" never think necessary. I, however, prefer those made out of plaited hemp or tow. They are merely a band of loosely plaited tow, about eighteen inches long, the heel rope being fastened to one end, and secured by a string or tape just behind the fetlock; they are much softer than the leather ones, and quite as strong. The disadvantage, however, is that they soon wear out, but they are very cheap; in fact, the "syces" can make them themselves out of the raw hemp or tow (sun). They are used by many of the native cavalry regiments in India in preference to the leather ones. The heel ropes can be made out of one long rope doubled, a "muzzuma" fastened to each free end, and the doubled portion to a tent-peg. When heel ropes are used, one should be put on each hind leg; it is dangerous to only put on one, and I have seen more than one fractured thigh caused by this. If the heel ropes are on both hind legs, and the horse kicks, he has to do so straight into the air, as there is equal restraint on both; but if there is only one, the unequal check of the single rope is likely to cause a fracture. If allowed, "syces" will always pull the heel ropes so tight as to stretch the horse out; they should be loose enough to allow him to stand in a natural position.

Head Ropes (*aghari*).

Head ropes should be fastened to the ring on the head collar (nukta) under the chin. There should either be two separate ropes, one end of each fastened to the ring, or one long one doubled in the middle, the central portion fastened to the ring, and the two ends to two wooden pegs driven into the ground about three or four feet on each side of the horse's head. If only a single rope is used, it must, naturally, be fastened to a peg straight in front, and, to allow the horse to move his head up and down, must be loose. When fastened in this way he is exceedingly likely to get his fore leg over the rope and get hung up in it, a nasty wound in the heel or at the back of the knee being the result, if nothing worse; whereas, if the ropes are pegged out on each side, he can move about freely, and it would be difficult for him to get his leg over them. Both head and heel ropes should be made of hemp; the cotton rope used in India for most purposes is not strong enough, and soon breaks and wears out. In Peshawur and along the north-west frontier, a rope is made of goat hair that is very strong, and is excellent for this purpose. It is somewhat more expensive than ordinary rope, but with care will last a long time, and will amply repay itself. Both head and heel ropes should be tied to the pegs in a slip-knot, so that with a single pull horses can be set free when necessary. "Syces" will usually tie them in a jam-knot, and horses struggling to get loose when frightened very often badly injure themselves before they can be set free.

Fetlock Picketing.

A method of picketing horses was introduced into the Indian army some years ago, by dispensing with head ropes and using a short chain shackle about three feet long, buckled round one of the fore fetlocks, and fastened to a peg driven into the ground. This was chiefly done with the object of reducing the weight carried, and with animals used for military purposes, doubtless fulfilled the purpose, but in a private stable I fail to see its advantages over the other plan.

Picketing Posts.

When horses are picketed outside the stable, and there is space enough, picketing posts are the most preferable method, as they allow greater freedom than any other. A stout smooth post, about five or six inches in diameter, is driven several feet into the ground, so that it is five or six feet above the surface, a strong iron ring is slipped over it, and to this the head rope is made fast; no heel ropes are used, and the horse can move round it as he pleases. The post must be smooth, so that there is nothing for the ring to catch in, and when put into the ground the point should be put into the fire and charred, or covered with kerosene oil, to keep off the white ants. It will also have to be examined occasionally to see that it is not damaged or rotten. The only drawback to this plan is that, if there are several horses, a considerable space is necessary, as they must be far enough apart to prevent their kicking at each other.

Ringing.

In South Africa and the colonies horses are picketed by the method known as "ringing," the head rope of one being fastened to the head collar of the next, and so on, till the head rope of the last is in its turn fastened to the head collar of the first, their heads forming a ring looking inwards. Colonial horses will stand like this for hours together; but they are very quiet, and behave in a different way to the Indian country-bred. I have seen the same plan used in a cavalry regiment of the Italian army on the march near Milan.

Rheims.

In South Africa head ropes are made of prepared raw hide called "rheims." They are prepared by the Kaffir women out of raw ox hide, and are very strong and supple, and are excellent for the purpose.

Knee-haltering.

Knee-haltering is also a South African plan of securing horses when turned out to graze. The fore leg is lifted up, so that the forearm from the elbow to the knee is parallel to the ground. The head rope, or "rheim," is then fastened above the knee, the head being pulled a little downwards. The horse is then turned out to graze on the veldt, and when his head is down feeding he can use his limbs and walk about as he likes, but as soon as he puts up his head to trot or gallop the fore leg is pulled up, and he has only three to go on, and can easily be caught.

Shackles (*bheri*).

The natives of India use iron shackles, much like handcuffs, to fasten with a key round both fore fetlocks of horses when turned out loose; but they are not a desirable invention, and in young animals are very likely to cause ringbones. But this, I think, is on account of their clumsy shape and being constantly worn, as I believe shackles made out of round iron that shut with a spring were used by the Canadian mounted police at one time when turning their horses out, and they found they did not chafe and rub so much as leather ones did. It was found that even moving through the wet grass the steel hobbles were polished, kept bright, and required no attention, whereas the leather ones perished and became hard, and gave constant trouble unless carefully looked after. I have never tried this plan myself, for I have found the Cape system of knee-haltering when turning animals out to graze the best I have yet come across.

Picketing-pegs (*make*).

Picketing-pegs should be made out of hard wood about eighteen inches to two feet long; iron ones are dangerous. They should be driven into the ground in a slanting direction, the point towards and the head away from the animal, to resist the strain on it. If there are no tent-pegs, or the ground is so soft that there is no holding for them, a hole a couple of feet deep can be dug, and a bundle of straw or a couple of tent-pegs tied crossways buried in it, the earth trodden down, and the rope brought out at the surface. This will give ample holding, and may be practically tested, for although a vertical pull will easily bring it up, the strongest man will fail to move it if the strain is horizontal.

Leading-ropes (*bagh durie*).

Leading-ropes are things that ruin half the horses' mouths in India, and I never let such a thing into the stable. If they are used as they were originally intended to be, that is, buckled into the ring of the snaffle or watering bridle to lead the horse with, they do no harm; but it is impossible to prevent "syces" from passing them over the head and then back through both rings, so as to form a gag, and this they hang on to. I always make them use a leading-chain, which is a leather strap with about a foot of chain and a snap-hook at the end of it. The hook fastens into the ring of the snaffle, and they cannot well pass the strap over the head to turn it into a gag. It seems impossible to teach a "syce" how to lead a horse in a watering bridle, and I find these chains the best compromise.

Brushes and Gear.

The grooming utensils required in an Indian stable are very simple: a horse-brush, curry-comb, bucket, some dusters, and a hoof-picker, being the sum total; but only one of these last is required among five or six horses. It is best to get English bristle brushes, they last out two of the native fibre ones, and are very little more expensive. Good horse-brushes are made by several firms in Cawnpore, and, of course, when a large number are used, the saving is considerable if the country-made article is bought, but where only a small number are required, this is a false economy.

Curry-combs.

These an Indian "syce" cannot get on without, and although he only uses it to wear out the brush, still, after all, it does not do so very much harm; but a bad, lazy man, if he is not prevented, will use it to scrape the dirt off the horse with. Country-breds are generally very thin-skinned, and feel the comb very much if scarified with it, as the "syce" is very fond of doing; and I am positive that this practice in many cases has to account for much of the proverbial bad temper of these animals. The curry-comb should never be put on the horse's body at all, and in reality it is useless. If it can be managed, it is best not to give the "syces" such things, the only use of them being to clean the brush with, and this can be done just as well with the palm of the left hand, and the brush does not wear out so quickly; but it is the custom to use the comb, and it is hard to prevent it.

Buckets (*balti*).

Buckets can be bought anywhere. Zinc ones are better than tin, although perhaps a little more expensive; one should be provided for each horse.

Dusters (*jharans*).

Dusters are things that native servants of every sort seem to consume in enormous quantities, and unless some check is put on it, the number used at the end of the month will be astonishing. Either the old one should be produced before another is given, or else some contract be given to them to provide them for themselves; but the former plan is the best; if the contract system is adopted, filthy rags will be used. They are luckily exceedingly cheap, and are made nearly everywhere.

Hoof-picker (*sum khodna*).

A hoof-picker can be made out of almost any piece of rod-iron, and one should be hung up in every stable. One for every four or five horses is enough.

Clothing (*gurdaine*).

In Northern India, if horses are not clipped they require in the winter at least two thick rugs, and if they are clipped an extra one, as the climate from November to the end of February is bitterly cold. The ordinary country clothing, made out of "mundah," and sold in the bazaars, called "jhools," keeps horses warm and answers its purpose, and is cheap—a rug of this material costing about Rs. 3; but I think myself that it is false economy to get it, and that the horse-clothing made at the Muir or Elgin mills at Cawnpore, or the Egerton mills at Dhariwal, in the Punjab, although perhaps at first somewhat more expensive, will in the end be found the cheapest, as with care one suit of this will last many years, whereas the country clothing is seldom much good after a second winter's wear. This clothing is made in all sorts of colours, and turned out in suits, and is every bit as good as English manufactured.

Country blankets (kumbal) can also be got; and the condemned soldiers' blankets, that are periodically sold by the military authorities, make excellent horse-rugs. I always think it best to get regular horse-clothing shaped and pieced out at the neck to buckle across the chest, or, at all events, to have one rug like this, even if the rest are ordinary square blankets, as the shaped clothing protects the front of the chest, which the square blanket will not do. The blanket can be used in the daytime, and the rug on the top at night, buckling across the chest, as leaving this part of the body exposed is a fruitful source of coughs and colds. Aprons, breast-pieces, and quarter-cords are seldom seen in India, except on race horses, and then only as a fancy matter.

Hoods (*khansilla*).

Hoods with hacks, harness horses, and polo ponies are not often required; but if horses are sensitive to cold, particularly if they are standing out at night, they are no doubt a great protection. They are made up of the same material as the country "jhool," and they also can be got to match the clothing made at any of the woollen mills. In any case it is a good thing to have a spare hood in the stable, even if it is not habitually used, as when a horse begins to cough if at once put on a severe cold is often averted.

Body-rollers (*paities*, or *farakis*).

Body-rollers are sold in the bazaar shops of native manufacture, but are most flimsy, and I strongly advise that either English ones, or else those made by any of the manufacturers of leather goods at Cawnpore, which are nearly as good as English ones, be used, although they may at first be a little more expensive. The common country rollers are always breaking, and never being properly stuffed, the webbing in the centre of the two pads presses on the ridge of the spine when the roller is buckled up. There is no more fruitful cause of sore backs than this, especially if horses are at all thin and standing out in the open. "Syces" have a trick of pulling up the straps of the roller as tight as possible, and if it gets wet with the dew or rain it shrinks up, and the tight webbing cuts and pinches the skin over the backbone, causing a sore back. With a properly made roller the pressure is taken on the sides of the back by the two pads, and the webbing does not come in contact with the skin at all. In any case, if the horses are standing out in the open at night, it is always advisable to go round the last thing and let the roller out a hole or two. If country rollers are used, direct pressure of the webbing on the spine can be taken off by putting a folded up duster or a handful of straw under it. If the back has been pinched or rubbed the roller should be left off, and the blankets or clothing kept in their place by a couple of tapes or pieces of string stitched to the edge of each and tied under the body.

Bandages (*puttie*).

Woollen bandages on the legs greatly add to the horse's comfort when standing out on a cold night. The ordinary ones sold in the bazaar answer well enough, only they are generally a little too wide and not long enough. The bandage should be put on commencing from below and finishing under the knee or hock, and not in the reverse direction, commencing above, as is often done. The tapes should be tied in a bow outside. What is known as the Newmarket bandage, made out of a semi-elastic woollen material, is an excellent one. It stretches somewhat when put on the leg, and gives it support. They, however, are somewhat expensive —about Rs. 4 a set—but with ordinary care will outlast several pairs of country ones. A good bandage is made by the Muir Mills Company at

Cawnpore out of the cotton webbing called "newar"; they are very cheap and good, but are not so warm as the cotton ones.

Summer Clothing.

This is rather a superfluity, and, unless with race horses, is not usually indulged in, for at the time it could be worn it generally is so hot that the less the horse has on him the better. Usually one of the blankets used in the winter is kept to throw over him when standing about, or when walking back from work. Drill summer clothing can be obtained at any of the woollen mills in India in a variety of patterns, or a native tailor (durzie) will make it up in your own verandah if you give him a pattern. At least two suits per horse are required, as it very soon gets dirty in the warm season and requires washing.

Eye Fringes (*makieara*).

Eye fringes are absolutely necessary in India, and are used in parts of Australia to protect the eyes from the flies. They are fastened on to the cheek strap of the head collar with a small tab and button-hole in place of a brow band, and have a fringe of either leather or cotton cords that hang down over the eyes halfway to the nose. I prefer the cord ones; the fringes are always flat and in contact with the face, whereas the leather ones are liable to curl up at the ends and allow the flies to get underneath. The cotton ones are easier mended than the leather.

Fly Whisks (*chaurie*).

I always give each "syce" a fly whisk to keep flies off the horse while at exercise, or when he is holding him anywhere. They are very cheap, last a long time, and if not provided, the "syce" will arm himself with a dirty duster or rag of some sort for the purpose. I may, perhaps, be too sensitive on this point, but to see a dirty rag flourished about an otherwise well-turned-out animal is to me a great eyesore.

Cleaning Horse Clothing, and Storing it in the Summer.

It never enters the head of a "syce" that clothing requires to be cleaned. It should be frequently hung out in the sun and well beaten with a stick, like a carpet is, and then well brushed on both sides with a stiff clothes-brush. If necessary, it should be laid out flat and scrubbed with a brush and soap and water, rinsed out with cold water, as hot will make it shrink, and then, when dry again, beaten and brushed. The straps on pieced rugs should have some dubbing (momrogan) now and again rubbed into them, to prevent their getting hard and the leather perishing. Summer clothing should be sent to the washerman (dhobie) to be washed. During the summer months woollen clothing should be first cleaned, and then folded up and put away, some camphor, pepper, and leaves of the "neem" tree, that grows in every garden in Northern India, being placed between the folds to keep off the moths. They should be folded away on the top of a box, board, or table, or somewhere raised off the ground, to be out of the way of the white ants, and once a week be unfolded and hung out in the sun to air for a few hours, folded up, and stored away again. There is no occasion to waste the spices that are with them; if they are carefully unfolded over some newspapers, the whole can be collected and used again.

Numdahs.

If used at all, felt numdahs should have a plain edge, and not be bound with coloured tape, as they so often are; particularly the cheaper ones, that are sold by native saddlers. I have frequently seen sore backs caused by this tape binding, as well as the hair in white horses discoloured by the edge. When put on, the numdah should be well pulled up into the arch of the saddle, particularly in front. The common practice is to put the numdah flat on the back, and then the saddle on the top of it, so that when the weight comes on it, the numdah gets tight and is stretched, and is a common cause of sore backs and galled withers. When taken off the horse's back, the numdah should be spread out in the sun to dry; it should then be beaten with a stick and brushed with a hard brush to get the dry caked perspiration out of it, and to bring the nap of the felt up again. If this is not done it will get as hard as a board, and neglected numdahs are certain to give sore backs. If the saddle is properly stuffed and fitted to the horse's back, a numdah is not required, the only use of it being to save the lining of the saddle, and for this purpose I prefer a leather one.

Grooming (*malish*).

Grooming is an art that native grooms excel in. They have infinite patience, and their long supple fingers are peculiarly adapted for the work. They, furthermore, are used to it, for every Oriental is an adept at shampooing or massage, constantly doing it to their own limbs and those of their friends. When the horse comes in from work the bridle should be taken off him, hung up on a peg, and a watering bridle put into his mouth, the stirrup irons run up to the top of the leathers, and the girths slackened. If there is a breast-plate it can be taken off, but the saddle should not be removed till the back gets cool. According to the season of the year, a light or warm rug should be thrown over the quarters, and the horse walked about till he gets cool. If there is much mud sticking on him, it can be rubbed off with a wisp of straw before the brush is used. Horses should not be washed, or, if they are, only under very exceptional circumstances, when specially ordered. It is, however, a favourite practice among "syces," as it saves a good deal of trouble; and it is much easier to wash off mud and dirt than to remove it with the brush, as ought to be done; they are also very apt to use the curry-comb for this purpose. When the horse is cool he should be gone over with the brush, to remove what dirt is remaining, and when this is finished the process should be repeated with the hands, the palm and bend of the wrist being used for this purpose. If it is the hot weather, the grooming had best be done out-of-doors; but in winter it is best to do it in the stable, as in Northern India there is a cold wind blowing even in the middle of the day, and if exposed to it horses are liable to catch cold. As soon as the grooming is finished, which with a clipped horse can be done in about half an hour, the clothing and bandages should be put on, and, if it is evening, the bed put down. Even if not worked, this process of grooming should take place twice a day—before the morning and evening feed.

Wisps and Grooming Pads.

Straw wisps or leather pads are particularly useful in developing the muscle of a thin animal, or bringing the skin into order when it has been neglected. The wisps are made by twisting some of the bedding straw together into a rope about three feet long. This is then doubled in the middle and again twisted, so as to form a flat pad. Two of these wisps are used, one in each hand, and they are alternately brought down with a slight slap and drawing motion in the direction of the hair, the whole body being massaged with them. It is sometimes a good plan, if there is much dirt in the coat, to cover the pad with a damp duster; the dirt seems to stick to it. This is particularly useful when horses are changing their coats; the hair sticks to the damp cloth, and the old coat is brought out quicker than it otherwise would be. The grooming pads are used in the same way. They are two circles of leather about four or five inches in diameter, joined together with a strip of chamois leather about three inches wide, so as to form a pad or cushion, that is stuffed with tow. On one side a piece of leather or webbing is stitched at each end, sufficiently loose to allow the hand to be slipped under it in the same way as the horse brush. Two of these pads are used, and the skin beaten or massaged by each hand alternately. Although, perhaps, at first horses are fidgety, when they get used to it they appear to enjoy it; and it has the advantage of letting the owner know, if he is not in sight, that the "syce" is working by the noise he makes.

Hand-rubbing.

If horses are inclined to get filled on swollen legs, the tendons should be well hand-rubbed for five minutes at each grooming hour. This hand-rubbing should commence from the lower portion of the limb and be continued upwards, not in the reverse direction, which is the usual practice. The limb should be lifted up, and the fingers worked with a kneading motion behind the tendons.

Washing.

The feet, mane and tail are the only parts that should ever be washed, unless specially ordered, and then as seldom as possible. When the feet are washed, great care should be taken that they are carefully dried afterwards, and bandages put on, as leaving the legs wet is one of the chief causes of cracked heels, more especially in the winter months, if there is a dry cold wind blowing. If soap is used, it should be soft-soap; or, better still, the soap nut, or "reita." This is a berry, the shell or outer covering of which, when soaked in water, swells up into a sticky mass, that lathers like soap, and by natives of India is used for washing purposes.

Uneven Manes.

When the mane gets ragged and uneven, it should be carefully brushed down four or five times a day with a damp water brush, to make it lie flat. The long hairs on the under side next the neck should be pulled out, so that the mane is thinned, and the lower part lies in a perfect curve along the neck. Some horses object, and are a little troublesome during this process; but, if it is done gradually, it can be easily accomplished. The long hairs in the mane should never be cut, unless it is intended to clip it off altogether, and make it into a "hogged" mane. If the mane will not lie down flat with an even sweep, it can be covered with a cake of mud for four or five days, when it should be removed, and renewed if necessary. Being dry, it will crack, and the pieces can be easily knocked off, and the dust brushed out. The mud cake generally has the desired effect after having been applied four or five times.

Hogged Manes.

The manes of polo ponies and cobs it is the fashion to "hog," or cut off close to the neck. It is best to leave the forelock, as it gives a certain protection against the flies and glare of the sun; also, to leave a lock of hair on the wither, to grasp with the hand when mounting. The best implement to hog a mane with is a pair of ordinary horse-clippers, but don't use a new pair, or they will get spoiled; old ones that are no use for the rest of the body, do well enough. It is best to sit on the animal's back when the mane is being hogged, and to cut forwards; the hair will be cut much smoother, and a neater job made of it than when standing on the ground at the side.

Ragged Legs.

If the horse is not clipped, the long hairs at the back of the legs look very unsightly. They should be pulled out, not cut off. If a little powdered resin is rubbed on the finger and thumb, the hair will stick to it, and come out much more easily, and the legs will have a smooth, even appearance, which can never be attained if they are cut off with scissors, no matter how carefully this is done; there will always be jagged ridges left. The long hairs under the jowl can be singed off by passing a lighted candle under the jaw once or twice. If the horse is at all frightened at the candle, he can be blindfolded; but the operation is so quick, that generally it is all over before he is aware of what is being done. The long hairs on the muzzle and chin can be clipped off with a pair of ordinary scissors. If the horse is not clipped all over, attention to these one or two little details make all the difference in his appearance, and in his being turned out smart, or the reverse.

Trimming Tails.

The tail should be grasped close to the root with one hand, which is run down so that the hairs are all gathered together, and a string or tape tied round below the fleshy part at the tip. The tail should then be drawn out straight, and the hair cut off with a single sweep of a sharp knife just below where the string is tied. The blade of the knife must be long enough to give a drawing sweep, which an ordinary pocket-knife will not do. There is nothing better for this than a sharp native sword, or "tulwar," as it is long enough to cut through all the hair at one stroke; or, failing a sword, a sharp carving-knife will do, the longer in the blade the better. Any uneven ends of hair that remain can afterwards be trimmed off with a pair of scissors; or, better still, by a pair of sheep shears. Tail-cutting machines are sold with an arrangement to fix the hair of the tail with a clamp, on which there is a sliding cutting-blade. These cut the hair off very smoothly and evenly; the only drawback is that they are somewhat expensive, costing about Rs. 16 in Calcutta or Bombay.

Clipping.

Arabs and many country-breds carry such fine coats that they do not require clipping, but most

Australians and colonials do; and if the coat is at all inclined to get long and thick, it certainly should be taken off, for horse-clothing is so cheap that an extra rug can always be got. Horses should not be clipped till the coat has "set," *i.e.* till the long winter coat has grown, and no more hairs will come off when the hand is rubbed over the skin. This is generally about the beginning of October in Northern India. They will generally require clipping twice or three times during the winter, or up to the middle of March. There are generally some professional clippers in every station, who bring their own clipping-machines, and charge about two or three rupees for a pony, and an extra rupee for a horse each time; or, if there is not such an individual about, permission can generally be obtained to have it done by any of the cavalry regiments in the station. It should be remembered that horses having just lost their coats will require an extra rug that night.

Cleaning the Sheath.

The owner must himself occasionally see that the horse's sheath is washed out. "Syces" never think this necessary, and the part gets into a filthy, dirty state, that in the summer months is likely to give rise to a troublesome sore, called a "bursattee" ulcer. Some horses are very troublesome to do this with, and it may be necessary to put on a twitch ("kinch mhal"); but this should always be done in the owner's presence.

Light in Stables.

With a new-comer, "syces" usually ask for oil to burn in a native earthenware lamp (charragh) at night, but it is a thing I never allow. In the first place, even if the lamp was kept burning, it is not required; horses rest better in the dark. In the second, it is dangerous with so much inflammable material about. In the third, the lamp will not be used in the stable, but the "syce's" own house. If a light is ever required, which is only on rare occasions, it is better to bring a lantern out of the house; and in India there is always a hurricane-lantern to be found in every house.

Fires in Verandahs.

"Syces" are very fond of lighting fires and making cooking places in the verandah of the stable, but this I never allow, as it litters the place up with cooking pots, and makes a great mess; also, it is dangerous. I always make them carry on their cooking operations in the verandahs of their own houses.

SADDLERY, HARNESS, CARRIAGES, AND SERVANTS.

Saddles (*zin*) and Harness (*saz*).

Saddles, harness, and all leatherwork requires a good deal more care and attention in India than in England, especially during the hot season, when the fierce dry heat will dry up and perish all sorts of leather; and in the rains, especially in Southern India, where the atmosphere is so loaded with moisture that leather, put on one side and neglected for a very few days, soon becomes covered with mildew. There are no saddle rooms in Indian stables, and it is usual to keep them in a corner of a room in the house on a wooden saddle-stand, called by natives a "ghorra" horse. In the rains, a pan or brazier of burning charcoal should be kept in the room for a few hours daily, if there is not a fire-place. Saddles are cleaned in the same way as in England, and excellent saddle soap and dubbing is made by the North-west Province Soap Works at Meerut, and can be obtained almost anywhere. If this is not used, the "syces" can always make up dubbing of their own, called "momrogan." Some people give their head "syce" a monthly allowance to provide dubbing, soap, bathbrick, oil, etc.; but as they frequently put lime and bleaching materials with it, I prefer to buy it myself, and let them get the other articles. They require a chamoise leather and a burnisher for steel-work, but one of each will do for a stable of half a dozen horses, and very good country-made leathers (sabur) can be got for from one to one and a half rupees. The soap is put on to and rubbed into leather-work with the hands; but the great fault they have is that they will put on too much, and won't work it in enough, and one's breeches and hands will get into a great mess.

Saddle Covers (*buk bund*).

A sheet, made out of a description of coarse country cloth (karwah), is necessary for each saddle or set of harness, to wrap it up in, and keep the dust and dirt off. It should be sufficiently large to wrap the saddle up in completely, and in the summer the "syce" can bring it with him to act as a horse-cloth to throw over the quarters when standing about.

These saddle-sheets can be made by any tailor in a few hours.

Bridles.

Bridles, double (dahna), snaffle (kazai), can be hung up on the walls, but a piece of cloth or a few sheets of paper should be fastened up behind them; and they should be frequently taken down if not in daily use, as the white ants are most destructive. It is best to have one or two extra saddle-stands made with pegs on them, and to hang the bridles on them in the middle of the room, away from the walls. This may be a little more expensive, but a saddle-stand can be brought for Rs. 5 that will hold a couple of dozen bridles, worth Rs. 20 apiece. At one time plated bits were used in India, but I think steel ones are the best. "Syces" never can tell the difference, and I have more than once found a plated bit being industriously scrubbed and polished with sand.

Harness.

Unless particularly desired, brown harness with brass mounts is the best—for India, at all events—for pony-harness, and it is this class of animal that is generally used in an up-country station. Not one "syce" in a hundred knows how to clean black harness properly, and if this is not done nothing looks worse, whereas almost any native can clean brown leather after a fashion, and even if it does not stand close inspection, it will pass muster at a little distance. Fairly good brown harness is made out of country leather, and it does well enough for rough work, but it never has the finish of English. Country leather reins and country bits should never be used; they are not reliable, and are most dangerous; these should always be English.

Carriages.

The ordinary two-wheeled pony-trap or dogcart, used in an up-country Indian station, is best varnished, not painted. The hot weather ruins paint, and, unless in some of the very large towns, it is nearly impossible to get them properly repainted again. Any native workman can, however, varnish a trap with white or copal varnish. Before allowing new varnish to be put on, the trap should be produced for inspection with the old scraped off, as it is a favourite trick to daub new varnish over the old, when it cannot properly set, and the first hot sun cracks and blisters it. In the hot weather a large earthen basin, called a "naund," should be kept full of water under the carriage in the coach-house; the evaporation of the water will keep the woodwork moist, and prevent its cracking with the heat. A matting made of the fibres of the "khus khus," or lemon grass, should also be put round the nave of the wheel, and kept wet, for the same purpose, as it is exceedingly likely to crack with the heat. The shafts of the trap should not be left resting on the ground, as they will warp and bend; they should be supported either by a wooden trestle, or else by a couple of ropes from the beams of the roof. The whip, when not in use, should be hung by a string at the upper part to a nail in the wall, and a weight, such as a brick, tied to the butt end to keep it straight; otherwise, in a very short time, it will get crooked.

Servants.

Indian "syces" are different to English grooms, as the new arrival will soon find. They have peculiar customs of their own, which, like all Orientals, they cling to tenaciously, and will not give up. If they are understood they are easily managed, and work well; but if not, the horse-owner's life is a burden to him, for no European can overcome the passive resistance of the Oriental.

In the first place, I never let any of the house servants interfere with the stable. Many persons, particularly those new to the country, do everything through their head servant, or "bearer"; but I make him stick to his own work, which is the control of the house and the house servants. I pick out one of the best and sharpest of the "syces," changing him till I get a good man, making him the head or "jemedar syce," and paying him a rupee a month more wages than the rest; and he is responsible for everything connected with the horses, and any small bills I pay to him, and him alone. The wages I pay myself to each man regularly on the seventh of the month, for the month previously. I never lift my hand to a servant, or fine him under any pretext, as the fine will only be made up out of the horse's grain, but, if fault has to be found, I do so in the presence of the head man; on the second occasion a warning is given, and on the third the offender is dismissed on the spot. I always keep a "syce" and a "grass-cutter" for each horse. It is possible to get a "syce" and two "grass-cutters" to look after two horses, by paying the "syce" a rupee a month more; but the arrangement is not satisfactory, although many do it. If the "syce" gets ill, which they often do, there is no one to do his work, whereas, if there is a man to each horse, they will arrange the extra work among themselves. In Northern India "syces" and "grass-cutters" should be provided with warm woollen clothes in the winter. An excellent cloth for the purpose is made by the various woollen mills, and at most of them servant's clothes can be bought ready made up; but it is best to give the men the materials and let them get them made up themselves, otherwise there is certain to be something wrong with them. A "syce's" coat costs about Rs. 4, and a "grass-cutter's," which is made out of a coarse blanketing, Rs. 3; and these coats should last for two winters' wear. In addition, I used to give each man a "coolie" blanket that cost Rs. 3, and which would last three winters; and, if they had to go out much into camp, such as taking horses out to meet me on shooting or pig-sticking expeditions, a pair of woollen leg-bandages, or "putties." It is a mistake not to give servants warm clothes, and a false economy, as, if they are not properly protected against the cold, which is very severe in Northern India, they are everlastingly getting fever; and I know no greater nuisance than having your head man laid up for two or three days at a stretch. In the second place, if they have not warm clothes themselves, you can never tell if in the night they will not take the clothing off the horses to wrap themselves up in. A constant source of squabbling amongst Indian servants is the allotment of their huts or houses. In the older Indian bungalows there is usually enough of both these and stabling, but in the newer ones there is not. It is best, however, not to listen to any such complaints, and somehow the disputants settle the knotty point themselves. Every now and again it is advisable to see who is living in your compound, as a most enormous number of relations will turn up, who are known as brothers (bhai); and if you don't look out, you will find you are giving shelter on your premises to several hundred individuals. Indian servants are always asking leave to attend weddings, funerals, and religious ceremonies; and I always allow them to go, provided some arrangement is made to carry on their work. They are clannish in the extreme, and a substitute was always forthcoming. In the hills "grass-cutters" are not required, as grass can be bought in the bazaars. The country people look on the sale of this as a vested right, and naturally resent any outsider cutting it or interfering with them; and, if they do, there is pretty certain to be a disturbance and unpleasantness. If "grass-cutters" are preferred to purchasing the daily supply, local hillmen should be employed, who will arrange the matter with their neighbours, and not men brought up from the plains of India. In most hill stations passes or licences have to be obtained to cut grass. In every Indian station there is an official price-list of country produce published, and should any dispute arise as to the rates charged, it is as well to obtain it from the native magistrate (tehsildar), whose decision in such matters is usually accepted as final, and which generally saves an immense amount of trouble.

SHOEING.

Shoeing (*nāl bundie*).

Shoeing is a subject on which a volume might be written of itself, far beyond the scope of this little work, and for further information on the art I would refer the reader to the treatises by Dr. Flemming and W. Hunting, Esq.; but as both these deal with European practice, I will only mention a few differences in the art as performed by the native smith, or "nāl bund." In most large military stations where there are European troops, permission can generally be obtained to have horses shod at the regimental forge, but in out-of-the-way places the native artist has to be employed. All horses require shoeing at least once a month, and some oftener, as with some the horn grows quicker than others, and the hoof requires to be shortened oftener. In these cases, if the shoe is not worn out at the toe, it can be replaced after the foot is shortened; this is what the English smith calls "a remove," the native "khol bundi." It is advisable after work to lift up the foot and look if the shoes (nāl) have shifted or not, also to examine the clench or point of the nail (preg) where it has been turned over, as it sometimes gets turned up and sticks out. If this happens on the inside of the hoof it is likely to cut the opposite fetlock (mawah lagna), and make a bad wound that may leave a permanent scar or blemish. Some horses, from bad formation, move their limbs so closely together that they always rub the fetlock joints when they move. This sometimes can be corrected by what is known as a brushing shoe; but some badly-shaped animals will always do it, no matter what sort of shoe is put on. Various forms of pads or brushing boots are sold to prevent this and protect the part; but, in my opinion, what is known as the Irish boot is the best. It consists of a thick piece of blanket, or "mundah," about six inches wide and the length of the circumference of the leg. This is fastened round the fetlock with a tape or string so that the ends are in the middle line of the leg behind, the upper half being doubled over the string so that there are two thicknesses to protect the fetlock joint. I have found this far better than the more elaborate contrivances sold; it is cheap—any one can make one in a few minutes—it does not collect mud and dirt like the others do, and it does not become hard like those boots made out of leather, which, unless carefully looked to and kept soft with soap (sabon) or dubbing (momrogan), are liable to cut horses badly. The only care required in putting on the Irish boot is not to tie it too tight, or the tapes may cut the skin. Some pieces of horn hanging loose, that are being cast off from the sole and frog in the natural process of growth, are often seen. These are very likely to collect dirt and moisture, and if they do they should be removed, but otherwise be left alone. They can generally be pulled off with the fingers, a piece of stick, or the hoof-picker. As a rule, in the plains of India the majority of horses do not require shoes on their hind feet, unless the roads are mended with stone, or the climate is very damp and the horn gets soft. In the rainy season, if much work is being done, they perhaps then require shoeing behind, but in the dry season the majority go just as well without. In the hills, where the paths are rocky and stony, horses, of course, require shoeing behind. Unlike the European, the native smith shoes what is called "cold," that is, he has a number of shoes in sizes from which he selects one as near a fit as possible, which he hammers into shape on a small anvil without heating it. Native shoes are generally perfectly plain, *i.e.* flat on both sides, and, unless specially made, are never "seated," *i.e.* sloped on the foot surface, or "bevelled," *i.e.* sloped on the ground surface. As a rule, the nail-holes are what the smith calls too fine, *i.e.* they are too near the outer rim of the iron, and to get a hold the shoe has to be brought back so that the horn projects over the iron. To obviate this the smith removes the toe with the rasp, thus weakening the horn at the very place where it is required to be strong. The shoes are generally somewhat too small also, and to get the nail to take hold they have to be set back in the same way as when the nail-holes are too fine. A native smith, unless he has been shown how, never knows how to turn down the point of the nail after it has been driven through the hoof to form the clench; he never cuts off the superfluous part, but turns it round in a curl with the pincers, and, needless to say, this is exceedingly likely to cause brushing. Another great fault is his fondness of pairing and slicing away the frog and sole, which he will have to be stopped in doing. I have seldom seen a horse pricked in shoeing by a native, but if left to themselves they never get the bearing true, and as a result corns are of common occurrence.

Of course, such light shoes as those of native manufacture have not a great lot of wear in them, and in heavy, holding ground would pull off, but on the hard level plains of India they last well enough, and the native smith, if his faults are known and corrected, is not a bad workman after his own lights.

GLOSSARY OF HINDUSTANI WORDS.

ADARWAH, *parched barley.*
AGHARI, *a head rope.*
AKH-TA, *a gelding.*

BAD HAZMIE, *indigestion, dyspepsia.*
BAGH, *rein.*
BAGH DORIE, *leading-rope.*
BAJARA, *millet seed.*
BALTI, *bucket.*
BANIAH, *corn-dealer.*
BĀNS, *bamboo.*
BHAI, *brother, relative.*
BHERIE, *iron shackles for horse's legs.*
BHESTIE, *water carrier.*
BICHALIE, *bedding straw.*
BUK BUND, *saddle sheet.*
BURRADAH, *sawdust.*

CHARPOY, *native bedstead.*
CHARRAGH, *native oil lamp.*
CHATTIE, *earthen pot.*
CHAURIE, *fly-whisk.*
CHEIL, *to dig up grass.*
CHICK, *split bamboo window blind.*
CHICK-NA, *muzzle.*
CHOKER, *bran.*
CHUCKIE, *hand-mill.*
CHUNNA, *gram.*
CHURRIE, *dried shorgum stalk used for cattle fodder.*
COMPOUND, *enclosure round an Indian house.*
CULTEE, *the black gram used as horse food in Madras.*

DAH, *a bill-hook.*
DAH-NA, *a double bridle.*
DAST, *diarrhœa.*
DASTOUR, *custom, percentage, perquisites.*
DHAN, *unhusked rice.*
DHA NAH, *grain.*
DHOOB, *an Indian grass on which horses are fed.*
DHOOL, *a small leather bucket used for drawing water.*
DURZIE, *a tailor.*

FARAKIE, *body-roller.*

GAJAR, *carrots.*
GEHUN, *wheat.*
GHORRA, *horse.*
GHORRIE, *mare.*
GUDDA, *donkey.*
GUMALO, *earthen vessel shaped like a milk pan, holding about a gallon.*
GUNNA, *sugar-cane.*
GURDAINE, *horse-rug.*

HAWAH, *air.*
HOOKHA, *a pipe.*
HURRIALIE, *a species of grass.*

JAI, *oats.*
JAMP, *a straw screen.*
JARU, *a broom.*
JHARAN, *duster.*
JHOOL, *country horse clothing made out of felt.*
JONK, *leech.*
JOW, *barley.*

KALI NIMUK, *black salt.*
KAR WAH, *a sort of cotton cloth.*
KAZAI, *watering or snaffle bridle.*
KHAL, *linseed cake.*
KHANSILLA, *hood.*
KHASIL, *green food.*
KHAWID, *green food.*
KHOALIE, *charcoal.*
KHOL BUNDIE, *a remove in horse shoeing.*
KHUA, *a well.*
KHUS KHUS, *lemon grass.*
KICHER KE MUTTEE, *clay.*
KINCH MHAL, *twitch.*
KIRIM, *worm, weevil.*
KUMBAL, *blanket.*
KURLIE, *manger.*
KURPA, *a short iron hoe, used to dig grass with.*
KUTCHER, *mule.*

MALISH, *grooming.*
MAKE, *a wooden tent-peg.*
MAKIE-ARA, *eye-fringe to keep off flies.*
MAUND, 80 *lbs. weight.*
MAWAH LAGNA, *brushing of the fetlocks.*
MISSA BHOOSA, *grain stalks crushed in thrashing.*
MOAT, *pulse grain.*
MOMROGAN, *dubbing.*
MOTE, *pulse grain.*
MUNG, *pulse grain.*
MUSSUK, *leather water-bag.*
MUTTIE, *earth.*
MUZZUMA, *leather heel-strap.*

NĀL, *a horseshoe.*
NĀL BUND, *a shoeing-smith.*
NAUND, *a large wide-mouthed earthen vessel holding several gallons.*
NEWAR, *cotton webbing.*
NIMMUK, *salt.*
NIRRICK, *the official price list.*
NUKTA, *head stall.*
NUMDAH, *felt pad for putting under a saddle.*

PAITE, *body-roller.*
PANI, *water.*
PECHARIE, *heel ropes.*
PREG, *nail.*
PUTTER KE NIMMUK, *rock salt.*
PUTTIE, *a roller bandage.*

RET, *sand.*
REITA, *soap nuts.*
RHAL, *linseed cake.*
ROLL KERNA, *to exercise.*

SABON, *soap.*
SABUR, *chamois leather.*
SAN, *a stallion.*
SAZ, *harness.*
SEER, *a two-pound weight.*
SHALGHAM, *turnip.*
SUFFAID BHOOSA, *wheat straw that has been crushed and broken in thrashing.*
SUM KHODNA, *hoof-picker.*
SUN, *tow or hemp.*
SYCE, *a groom.*

TOBRA, *a nose-bag.*
TOKAR, *to trip or stumble.*
TOKRIE, *a basket.*
TULWAR, *a curved native sword.*

ULSIE, *linseed.*

ZIN, *a saddle.*